Sound Friendships

Sound Friendships

The story of
Willa and her hearing ear dog

BY
ELIZABETH YATES

The Countryman Press
Woodstock, Vermont

Library of Congress Cataloging-in-Publication Data

Yates, Elizabeth, 1905–
    Sound friendships.

    1. Hearing ear dogs.   2. Hearing ear dogs—Training.
I. Title.
HV2509.Y37   1987   636.7'088   86-29110
ISBN 0-88150-080-1

Text and jacket design by Dede Cummings

Printed in the United States of America

Sound Friendships

Introduction

WHAT IS A HEARING EAR DOG? Fifty years ago the question might well have been asked, "What is a Seeing Eye Dog?" Now, bred and trained to guide blind persons, Seeing Eye Dogs are seen on city streets and college campuses, in stores, offices, planes, and buses. Familiar and respected for what they are and do, they give independence and mobility to individuals for whom loss of sight has meant severe limitations. Now, Hearing Ear Dogs are giving to the deaf independence and security that compensate in some measure for their deprivation.

The first Hearing Ear Dog was introduced in 1975 by Agnes McGrath, a Master Trainer. She was asked by the Minnesota SPCA to do a feasibility study to determine whether dogs could be trained to aid the deaf. She proved that they could with six carefully trained dogs. After she demonstrated what these dogs could do for deaf people, the first training center was established under the auspices of the American Humane Society in Denver, Colorado. In time, other states started such centers and today there are about thirty functioning programs across the United States.

The American Humane Society no longer operates a training center, but it has established "The Hearing Dog Project," which serves as an information and advocacy center offering a nationwide referral service. Two recent symposia, one in San Francisco, the other in Boston, have brought hearing dog program specialists together to discuss national guidelines, identification for the dogs, and training procedures.

Agnes McGrath's hope was that a time would come when Hearing Ear Dogs for the Deaf would be as recognized as guide dogs for the blind. Her hope has been partially realized: assurance came when the Colorado legislature passed a law that dogs trained and certified as Hearing Ear Dogs be accepted in all public places and conveyances. One state after another—except Hawaii and Alaska—has enacted similar laws. The federal government gave its recognition when the Internal Revenue Service ruled that expenses incurred for such dogs were tax deductible.

During their first decade of service, Hearing Ear Dogs have proved the merits of their worth by assisting some three thousand hearing-impaired people. Alerting their masters to sounds in their environment, as well as becoming the visual sign of their deafness, these dogs have become a valued tool to educate the public about this invisible handicap that affects more than sixteen million Americans.

The concept of Hearing Ear Dogs and the credibility of their use as a support system for the hearing impaired has become more widely known and accepted during the past two-year period. This awareness is the result of intense efforts by our program (and all Hearing Ear Dog organizations) to educate the public. These efforts have included articles in national publications, television exposure, demonstrations to civic groups, and, most importantly, the example of our graduates themselves who use their Hearing Ear Dogs for independence and security in their daily lives.

And now we have this perceptive and inspiring book by Elizabeth Yates, whose insights reveal the bonds that quickly grow between one of our dogs and its owner, opening the human's life to enhanced fulfillment.

The people and dogs in this account might have been those at any one of the centers functioning across the United States. Although there are minor differences in procedure, the common elements of staff commitment and dedication pervade all. The almost spiritual happening that occurs when a deaf person and dog are matched to become a team is a scenario that is duplicated at all centers. The shared qualities of special communication, mutual love, and loyalty are demonstrated by these teams regardless of where or how they have been trained.

Elizabeth Yates made frequent visits to the center at West Boylston, Massachusetts, to observe first the training of the dogs, then their matching. Conversations with the new owners and interviews with people who had had dogs for several years, gave her much of the material with which she has told her story. With rare understanding of the mind of the dog and sensitive insight into the problems of deafness, she has captured the essence of this coming together of need and service, which to us at the center always seems to be a kind of minor miracle. Into the warp of facts she has woven the woof of a story that has touched us all.

Sheila O'Brien, Executive Director
Hearing Ear Dog Program
West Boylston, Massachusetts

One

IT HAPPENED IN A MOMENT OF TIME, and because of it all the moments of life were different. A firecracker tied to a pigtail made a shattering sound: the last Willa was ever to hear. But that had happened more than ten years ago, when she was fourteen, and she had become used to her limitation. She had learned skills that helped her through school, then into business school, where a practical course assured her work as a secretary, with sight serving her and hearing not essential.

She could remember and hold in her mind much that had been the music of life—wind in the trees, laughter of children, her name being called; and there were things she did not want to remember—the many operations, her head swathed in bandages, the visits to specialists, and the faces of her parents. The fact that remained was the same after a year as it had been at the moment: the otic nerve had been destroyed, even a hearing aid would not help. Speech reading and sign language would give her means of communication with others, and a small device implanted in her ear would enable her to keep her own voice modulated.

During her years of growing up, Willa was protected by her parents, almost overprotected, as in their anguish they tried to make up for what she had lost. At twenty-five, alone and in new surroundings, she faced the self she would live with the rest of her life. The house had been too big, too much to keep up after her father died and then her mother, so she had moved to a ground-floor apartment that had a small backyard. It would be nice for Poppy, who was getting to be an old dog, and Willa would have a place to grow some flowers.

"You'll make out all right," people had said in their well-meaning ways, writing it in letters as they were more sure of the written word getting through to her. "You have all along. Living by yourself is just one more thing to get used to. Let us know when we can help. Give yourself time."

Oh, they were all so kind, but did they know, could they ever really know, what it was like to live walled into a world without so much as a whisper to penetrate its silence?

Poppy seemed to understand when Willa talked to her, but people often became so irritated, raising their voices as if that would help. Willa knew she was slow at speech reading and her lack of immediate response would cause annoyance. Because she could converse, people forgot and thought she could hear and would call to her on the street. It was no use, unless they waved or gave a visible signal. Acquaintances began to fall away and a friend explained, "They think you're snobbish. They just don't understand."

Willa withdrew more and more into herself, building a wall of suspicion. She thought people were talking about her because they could not talk to her. As her links with the present fell away, she read more, found interest in cooking, and planted flowers that gave fragrance. She could see, she told herself, taste, smell, and she could touch Poppy and feel a response. Sometimes it seemed that they did not look at each other so much as into each other, sharing their peculiar quiet.

TV meant little except that it gave Willa practice in speech reading; and there were some programs, generally foreign ones, that had captions below the pictures. One evening, when watching the news, Willa's attention was arrested by a scene of dogs working with people in a large open field. They were not show dogs but a curious mixture of breeds ranging from small to large. They were not Seeing Eye Dogs either, for they were on long leashes instead of harnesses. There was something about the people that looked familiar to Willa. She knew how a person with impaired hearing tended to walk, cautiously, turning the head frequently from right to left, often using the shadow cast by an approaching pedestrian to edge more to one side. But these people were walking with more confident strides. They were in an open field and each one led a dog on a yellow leash. Then a caption came on.

These were dogs that had been trained to function as ears for their deaf owners. Willa watched more intently. When the hour came to an end, the name of the Hearing Ear Dog program was given, the address, and interested viewers were urged to write for information. Willa wrote a letter. She rarely went out at night as darkness compounded her need to watch sharply for traffic, but caution balanced by a surge of hope overcame the fear that had been a safeguard. Her heart heard the thud made by the letter as it was dropped into the box.

An answer came soon and its warmth assured Willa that there were people ready to help and provide a way out of her prison. She might, indeed, qualify for a dog and an application form would be sent to her. The first exchange of letters was followed by others. It was understandable that they would want to know her age, health, work, but she wondered why it was important for them to know her feeling about animals. She had grown up with the family dog as she told them. She found it comforting to write about Poppy, knowing they would understand what she had meant to her for many years.

Poppy had always been there, fed by whomever happened to be in the kitchen near feeding time, responding to whomever called if she had a mind to, enjoying being petted when deserved. But as for making much of her, it was no more than making much of a piece of furniture; and yet, after the explosion, Willa remembered that something had begun to deepen between herself and Poppy. It was as if they needed each other, the one who did not speak, the other who did not hear. When Poppy died, Willa cried as she had never cried for herself. Now there was to be another dog in her life, a dog trained to meet her needs and with whom she would have to train.

The outreach worker from the regional Hearing Ear Dog program came to call on Willa. Communication developed easily between them through speech reading and signing.

"We've been working with this particular group of dogs for three months and we know a good deal about them, their personalities, their temperaments. They are as different as people. Now we need to know about you so we can match a dog to you, for our satisfaction is in the perfect match."

The worker described the dogs and the screening they had gone through before they were accepted for training. After training they would be certified as Hearing Ear Dogs. "Now, by law, these dogs are permitted to accompany their deaf owners to any place, in any conveyance, in all states except Alaska and Hawaii. Identification is established by their yellow harnesses and leashes with the words in big black letters HEARING EAR DOG. The owner carries ID as well."

"Those were the dogs I saw on TV."

"Some of them."

Excitement and eagerness tumbled out in the questions Willa asked and to which the worker responded.

"They are strays for the most part, obtained from animal shelters, and many have behind them stories of neglect and abandonment. Because of their need for love they seem to have a special capacity to respond to love. A few come because an owner is going away and must find a home, or from a breeder who has a misfit. They are a motley lot and it is not easy to identify breeds. You may see the dominance of a spaniel or collie, a lab, a hound, a poodle in ruff or tail or color, but often there is no clue at all."

Willa spoke of the pint-sized poodle she had noticed on the TV show.

"That's Molly, a peekapoo, white as a snowdrift and weighing all of ten pounds. She was found walking down a city street, obviously abandoned as no amount of searching discovered an owner, but she was responsive to training. She has been our 'demonstration dog' for six years. 'Molly gives lectures' they say at the office about her as she goes with the instructor or one of the trainers to clubs and organizations to show what a Hearing Ear Dog can do and to enlist support. Molly would never do for you."

"No, I would like a knee-high dog whose head my hand could rest on."

"A gentle dog with outgoing ways. A dog with a sense of humor, perhaps?"

Willa smiled suddenly. "You seem to know my needs."

"Let me tell you the procedure. When strays are found they are taken to the animal shelter, fed and washed, and an attempt is made to discover the owners. When we are ready to train a new group of dogs we visit the shelter to screen the ones recently found to determine their potential as working animals. For our purposes they should be young, from eight months to two years old, and range in size from small, like Molly, to about forty-five pounds.

"They are all appealing. Most of them have already been house-trained and had some experience of life. We can soon tell which ones may be suitable for the program and these are then taken to a veterinarian who keeps them in quarantine for two weeks and verifies their ages by the soundness of their teeth. They are spayed or neutered, given a thorough health examination to be sure there is no latent disease or problem, x-rayed, and given all their necessary shots. When the vet pronounces them hale and ready, we bring them to our kennels to start them on a training period that will last for three to five months. During this time of working and testing the trainers discover a great deal about their personalities and temperaments."

Willa wanted to know more. It was hard for her to believe that there could be such differences in dogs. "What are they tested for?"

"Willingness to work: fetching an article, for instance, and doing it not for fun or on impulse, but at the trainer's command. Curiosity: and that is synonymous with intelligence. Ability to localize sounds: any dog will alert to a sound, but finding where it comes from is something else. Seeing an image in a mirror will reveal something, as will reaction to a clockwork toy released across the floor, or the rippling notes from a harmonica. A hair gently pulled may cause a sharp snap and a baring of teeth or a mere turning of the head toward the one whose hand was given to stroking. The tests show us whether a dog wants to please, and this is essential; energy, self-confidence, stability are all essentials, too. Always there is the question underlying everything: Is this a dog that can accept responsibility? The tests are hard and constant through the time of training, and only one dog out of four passes."

Surprise and puzzlement were on Willa's face. "Why?" was on her lips.

"One day a dog may be good at sounds, the next day it couldn't care less, and it has to be good every day. Getting to know the dogs as they work with them, the trainers have learned to love them as they love in return. So, if some fail the program everything is done to find homes for them where responsibility is second to companionship."

"It must make demands on love."

"Yes, and money. Months are involved in the care and boarding, first at the vet's then in our kennels during the training. With our program the cost is $2150 a dog. Few applicants are able to pay that much, so sponsors are needed. Clubs, organizations, businesses, sometimes individuals stand ready to help. Every student coming to the program is asked to pay $150 for his or her dog. Does this alarm you?"

"Not yet, but I was wondering if I would pass your test to be deserving of such a dog."

"You have already, in your obvious need and in what you have told us about Poppy. You already have a sponsor. When you gave us your place of business as a reference, we wrote them about the program and your interest in it. They agreed to be your sponsor."

"Oh!" Willa exclaimed, "How good of them. And the dog, what kind will you choose for me?"

"I have a picture to show you. We think you and Honey will be a good match."

Then Willa held in her hand a snapshot. "A golden retriever," she breathed, scarcely able to utter the words.

"Not quite. Honey's grandparents were probably purebreds but her father was a man about town."

"It doesn't matter."

"Of course not! When you meet her you'll see the best of the known and the unknown strains in her."

"When! Yes, when?"

Willa was given the date for the new class and information as to where it would be held. "You have plenty of time to make your arrangements."

Time! Referred to as needed again but now not something to be endured, lived through, but something where every moment would count. At her office she asked for and received a month's leave of absence, then she made her preparations. Letters were written to friends to explain where she would be and what she would be doing "for my vacation." A visit was made to the bank, books were returned to the library, a few purchases were made—one of them an alarm clock—and suitcases were packed.

When she closed the door of her apartment behind her it was with a sense of subdued excitement, knowing that the next time she opened that door she would not be alone. Someone would be with her, someone who was to be a part of her life. She went to the bus station and bought a round-trip ticket.

Of her two suitcases, the larger was the lighter. It contained the blanket she had brought to be Honey's bed, a six-foot webbed leash, and the alarm clock she had been told to bring.

There were six in the class and they met that first afternoon knowing nothing about each other but having one thing in common that united them before they knew each other's names. Four had degrees of impairment that enabled them to wear hearing aids, all could speech read to an extent and some could sign; one other besides Willa was profoundly deaf. Willa was the only one from New England; others had come from much farther away. They met with smiles and shaking of hands, the universal language.

"When will I get my dog?" was the question each one asked the instructor. They had all seen pictures and been given descriptions of their dogs, and each one had the required six-foot leash ready to be attached to a collar.

"Tomorrow. We have a lot to do today."

Each student had been given a folder with papers to be studied and some to be signed, the most important and immediate was the contract entered into with the program.

CONTRACT

I, the undersigned, hereby agree to take full responsibility for the continuous care and training of the hearing ear dog I obtained from "The Hearing Ear Dog Program."

I understand that the program can decertify the dog with no reimbursement to me or my contributing sponsors in the event that the dog is abused or neglected or not being used for the purpose for which it was trained.

SIGNATURE _____   DATE _____

There were other papers with questions to be answered, but the instructor said that they could be done during the evenings of free time. Willa felt as if she had gone back to school, which, in a way, she had.

A sequence of slides was then shown. They told the story of a woman coming to the program to get a dog, the words of the sound track supplemented by the instructor's signing. The students were asked to imagine themselves in the place of the woman on the screen, for what she did they would soon be doing.

"Don't be surprised when you meet your dog tomorrow if you are ignored. 'You're not my trainer, what have I got to do with you?' the dog is thinking, but the trainer is not near and you are. There is a whole new relationship to be established and that is where your long leashes come into use. Snapped on to the chain-link training collar at one end and the other end tied to your belt, it is like an umbilical cord. For the first few days your dog will be with you at all times. Only when you go to bed or take a shower will you release the connection. This is bonding. During it the dog becomes an extension of you. You will feed the dog at the same time every day in your own room, you will walk with your dog, and you will discipline your dog. That first look you were given of avoidance will change to one of complete trust. This may not happen with you tomorrow, but you can see it happening with the woman on the screen and it will be the same for you. Relationships deepen through days of training, and when it is time for you to leave you and your dog will know that you have become a team."

An early supper followed and then they were dismissed for the night. Each one had work to do, and for all of them morning could not come soon enough, the morning when they would be matched with their dogs.

Willa sat at her desk, reading and then answering the questions on the sheets given her. Some of them seemed elementary, but there were others that caused her to search for the right answer, then admit that she really would not know until the instructor had taken them further through the course. Looking ahead to Honey and the routine that would be hers as a working dog, she thought back to Poppy and the casual life she had led. The door would be opened and she would go out, staying as long as she liked and returning when she pleased, no one knowing or caring where she went or what she did, except for the last year when her range had been the garden. Honey's life would have a definite pattern and it would be up to Willa to maintain it.

She put the papers back in their folder and got ready for bed. She would read for a while; the book that had been recommended to the class that afternoon was *How To Be Your Dog's Best Friend* by the Monks of New Skete. She read until sleep began to take her over, then she put out the light and reached down to smooth her hand over the blanket on the floor by her bed. "Good night, Honey." It was easy to pretend for one more night. Tomorrow Honey would be there.

It was only a short distance across an open field to the kennels. Once there, the students were told to wait outside, their dogs would be brought to them. One after another they came—Laddie, an almost collie; Cookie, a small dog that said something about a romance between a beagle and a spaniel; Emily, a lab with a trace of husky; Ebony, black, smooth-haired, stately and quite unidentifiable; Jack, a white shepherd with droop ears; and Honey. Trainers led them to their new owners, showed how the link collar should be put on and the long leash attached. The dogs were more interested in their trainers than in the people to whom they were led, but after leashes were attached to collars and trainers withdrew they seemed to realize that a new thing was happening. Some barked for attention, others jumped against the strange legs, and some circled in a whirl of uncertainty.

For Willa, time that had been enemy and ally stood still. She was aware of a tug at her heart like the tug Honey was making on the leash; then she reached down and drew the leash in. She laid her hand on the golden head. Surprised, Honey looked up at her. A warm soft tongue caressed the new hand, and in that moment a transfer of affection was

made. Willa looked away quickly. Had she been alone she
would have let tears flow, but there was too much to attend
to and the instructor was speaking.

"Call your dogs by their names. Go off with them across
the field for a few minutes. Let them get to know who you
are."

One walked sedately. Two ran in circles, tangling leashes
and legs, another sat down in puzzlement; the shepherd pulled
hard, wanting to run. Honey leaned against Willa, raised her
head again, and their eyes met and held. A trainer approached.

"You don't need to go across the field if you don't want to.
You've made eye contact and that is most important of all.
There's no question in Honey's mind that she belongs to you
and you belong to her."

When the others returned, the first lesson was given. "Tie
your leashes to your belts and we'll begin work." That was
back at the house. Sitting down in the big room, the dogs
were put in a down-stay position and the students listened
to the instructor. There were no slides this time, just words
clearly spoken and signing to supplement.

"Your dogs have had three months of obedience training,
and they know the basic commands–heel, sit, down, stay,
come. Their vocabularies will increase with specific needs as
you work with them. *Tell* is a fairly new word, so is *fetch*, and
you will use them both in time. *No* means business, and it
will be most effective with your facial expression of displeasure
and the shakedown."

"What's that?" someone asked.

"It's what a mother dog does with her puppies when she
wants to teach them a lesson they'll not forget." The instructor
took the dog nearest her, put both hands on the scruff of the
dog's neck, looked intently into the eyes gazing at her, and
shook the dog, not roughly or hurtfully, but so the meaning
was manifest. "Gently does it, every time."

The trainer's glance went around the group to be sure she

had their attention. "Another command will be given, not by you but by the situation and that is *think*. While walking with your dog on the street you may be surprised that instead of heeling as it has been doing, your dog sits down and refuses to move. What sound has come to those attentive ears, what warning? When you turn and see a car approaching from behind, you will know that danger has been averted.

"Don't question your dog. Act. You have been giving commands that have been faithfully followed, but there will be times when your dog may give you a command. Reward with praise and a great show of affection. Your dogs want to please you, but let me warn you that they are smart—if they weren't they wouldn't have been chosen for the program—and they'll test you sometimes in ways of their own devising."

That afternoon they went back to the field to practice the commands and learn the hand signals that went with them. Repetition was constant, but through it the dogs learned the tone of new voices, the feel of new hands. Some might still look longingly at their trainers who stood at a distance, but gradually all gave full attention to the ones beside whom they walked. Later in the big room the dogs settled down comfortably by their owners, finding six feet of leash sufficient freedom. Some licked their paws and other parts of their bodies, most flattened out in sleep.

"At all times," the instructor began, "your dog must know that you are the boss. Reward good behaviour with little treats and praise, then with praise only. Accept the paw that is offered you, stroke the head that leans against you. This is body language and it means more than words. Oh yes, these dogs can misbehave, and you will have to know how to deal with their mistakes, or sometimes worse." Her eyes swept the class. "Does this surprise you?"

Heads nodded.

"All right, let's say that your perfectly house-trained Cookie makes a puddle on your best carpet. Don't call Cookie. Go and get her. Show her what she has done, pointing your finger and looking displeased; give her the shakedown and let her have a moment to think things over while you mop up. Then put your arms around her and love her as if she were the dearest dog in the world, which she is. Chances are she won't wet again unless there's a physical problem; in that case you should take her to the vet. What if Laddie tends to bark at callers? Anticipate behaviour, and when you see him just thinking about barking, stop it before it happens."

"How?"

"Get down to his level, take him by the scruff of the neck and give him a shakedown. Look at him sternly, point your finger at the door, shake your head and say, 'Don't you dare, don't you dare.' or something equally meaningful to him. And that brings up another point of behavior I want you all to be sure of: there is no excuse for aggression *ever*, and you can curtail any tendency toward it by anticipating it and warding it off. Understand?"

One after another heads nodded as each one became increasingly aware of all that ownership of a Hearing Ear Dog involved.

"You will soon learn of your dog's inner timing, and you will be told in no uncertain way when to go out is a necessity, but should you slip up and should it happen in a public place, be prepared. Always carry a plastic bag and a little scoop, pick up the poop and dispose of it properly. It is the law and both you and your dog must respect it."

While the instructor was talking, Emily had been inching herself toward the table and a doughnut that had been left there. Her nose could just reach it, then a paw was lifted toward it, but before the tempting morsel was in her mouth her owner saw her and drew in the leash sharply.

"Don't you dare," she said, removing Emily from the doughnut, "don't you dare even to think of such a thing."

"Now what do you do?" the instructor asked.

"Love her."

"Yes, after the misbehavior has stopped and when you are

sure she has learned her lesson. She won't try to sneak food again if you are on the watch."

While Emily was receiving her due of affection, the instructor turned to Willa. "What if Honey does something bad like getting up on the couch you have just had recovered and that she has been told is not for her?"

Willa looked puzzled and shook her head. She could not imagine Honey ever doing anything wrong; she could not see herself ever having to rebuke her.

"You'll say *off*, sternly, quickly, and you may have to use the shakedown just that once to impress her. Don't say the word down, as that is one of the commands she has learned, say 'off,' then reward her with praise. Tell her she's a good girl and that you love her."

The instructor looked around the group, again gathering the attention of everyone. "In their enthusiasm your dogs may jump against you and unless you nip that tendency you'll have a real problem with your friends and anyone who comes to your house. All right, let's say that Jack's paws are suddenly on my chest and he is about to kiss me with that great lolling tongue. I'll bring my knee up against his chest with enough force for him to feel it and I'll say, 'Don't jump.' The message will get through if you are quick enough. Discipline is always done from love, with love, but remember that sometimes love has to be tough."

Five o'clock was feeding time for the dogs. Students were given bowls, shown where the food was and told the amounts the dogs were accustomed to; then, with bowls filled, they went to their rooms, closed their doors, and let the dogs eat. Time was allowed for a rest, then a walk. Later, when the students gathered around the table for their supper, the dogs were given the down-stay command; some went under the table, some settled near chairs, tucking their noses between their paws. It did not appear necessary, but the instructor gave a precaution, "Never feed your dog from the table, and never rich food. They function best on their own diet."

That night in her room with Honey asleep at her feet, Willa reviewed the Basic Obedience sheet. The words had become familiar and she read them with a smile of remembrance, recalling what Poppy had done without anybody taking the trouble to teach her anything, and what she had not done. All those commands, beginning with "heel" would have been meaningless. Poppy had walked wherever she liked, ahead, behind, beside, and then disappeared on adventures of her own. Hand signals! Poppy would have thought them a game, but with these dogs they were a form of language. Poppy would have liked the praise and the embrace that followed the exercises whether she deserved such or not, but with these dogs praise had to be earned, then it was given lavishly.

There was a sheet with instructions about getting in and out of a car with your dog. Willa stared. Her father had taught her to drive years before she was old enough to have a license, but after the explosion she had wondered if she would ever have a license and had talked herself into thinking she would never drive a car, yet something in her had kept the feel of a wheel in her hands, the place where her foot went for clutch or brake. Now, reading the instructions, she knew that she could have a car someday, for Honey would give her more than confidence; she would give her the warning necessary for decisive action in an emergency.

Willa imagined herself sitting at the wheel with Honey beside her, interested, alert, nose quivering. When traffic flowed normally, signals were obeyed and road signs heeded, they would go freely about their business. Let a siren sound in the distance, Honey would hear it, put her front paws on Willa's right shoulder and keep them there until Willa had pulled to the side of the road and come to a halt. Once fire engine, ambulance, or police car had zoomed by and traffic resumed its flow, Honey would sit upright on the seat again. It was the uncertainty that made Willa fearful, but a copilot could make a safe driver even safer. So into her future moved the shape of a car.

She began to think of other aids—a telephone with TTY equipment that writes the message when the phone is answered; Honey would alert her to answer the phone. And there was something else that had nothing to do with Honey but that might be possible—a closed caption device to be attached to her TV screen so she could read what she could not hear. But Honey would be in on this too. Willa would not leave the room wondering if she had turned the TV off. If she had not, Honey would soon tell her and send her back to it. There were so many things Willa had told herself she would never be able to do. Now, never had become perhaps. She quivered with inner excitement. It was like the feeling at Christmas when hands were held till the time came to open a package whose contents were known and longed for but not to be revealed until the moment came.

Honey's presence in the room gave a new meaning to life. They had communed together as two with a common bond, and though Honey was now asleep, head between paws and body relaxed, Willa's thoughts went on. She seemed to be looking at herself as she had not done for a long time, facing herself without embarrassment or apology. True, she could not hear, but she could feel a nose when it pushed itself into her hand for attention, she could see eyes that looked into hers and spoke of things too deep for words, she could smell clean fur. What was it the psalmist had said, "Taste and see that the Lord is good." Yes, she could taste and acknowledge the goodness. Four senses: she had consoled herself with that number for a long time, but it had taken a dog to bring her to their realization.

She dropped her hand to run it over Honey. One eye opened, the head lifted slightly, but it was clear there was to be no command, no need. The head dropped back on the blanket, the tail moved, a sigh twitched through the body, then sleep was resumed. Willa put her head down on her pillow. Once she had resigned her heart to loneliness; now it rested in companionship.

"Auditory awareness" was the professional term, but "work on sounds" was more explicit, and this followed as well as included the lessons on obedience. It was individually done —one trainer, one student, one dog. Willa was taken into a large, sparsely furnished room. There was a cot with a table beside it and, some distance away, a chair and another table. The alarm clock Willa had brought with her was set, placed on the table by the cot, and she was told to get under the covers and feign sleep. The trainer sat down across the room and started to look at a magazine. Honey, free to do what she liked, investigated the room. Suddenly the alarm went off. Honey raced across the room, placed her paws on the cot, and tugged at the blanket. She kept tugging until Willa responded and sat up, wide awake. She told Honey what a good girl she was, and Honey's tail wagged pleasure at her accomplishment and the treat that had been slipped to her.

There came a knocking at the door. Honey, without so much as a glance at Willa, raced to the door but did not stay at it. She ran back across the room to Willa, looked at her and raced again to the door. She did this several times until she convinced Willa that the door was to be opened. Someone stood there, another trainer, but Honey restrained her enthusiasm to stand beside Willa, looking up at the one from whom approval would come. When the smoke alarm went off Honey looked startled. She hesitated a moment then went to it and raced back to Willa. "Honey, tell," Willa said, the word she had been told to use. Honey pushed against Willa and nudged her toward the door, indicating that this time they both must go out the door.

"Well done," the trainer nodded.

"I never seem to ask anything of Honey," Willa said.

"No, you don't ask, you tell, and that means for her to do it. The sounds we have just practiced are the first that every Hearing Ear Dog learns. There are others, and some for particular people. Any sound that could mean danger Honey will alert you to. It may mean nothing at all, but to her it is something you should know about. Cookie will be taught to respond to a baby's crying, as Cookie's owner has a small baby at home; Emily will respond to a kettle boiling. Tomorrow when we go out for a drive, you will see how Honey reacts to road sounds—a fire siren, an ambulance, a police car—and tells you of them.

"Some dogs have to be trained for very unusual sounds. In our last class there was a man from a part of Texas where rattlesnakes abound. His dog learned the warning sound made by a rattler, looked in its direction but did not go to it. It was the turn of the head that told the dog's owner there was something to be avoided in those tall grasses or that pile of rocks."

"However did you have a rattle, handy?"

"We sent to Texas for one, so it was genuine enough. Is there something in your way of living that requires a certain sound?"

Willa could think of one, her own name. "Could Honey learn to respond to it when people call to me? So often they wonder why I don't answer."

"Of course," and the rest of the time was spent on that.

First the trainer said "Willa" while pointing to the person, then Willa said her name and pointed to herself. The exercise was repeated until Honey went easily to Willa when she heard her name said.

In a pause from working, Willa spoke of something that troubled her. "How will I know that I am using the right tone of voice when talking to Honey?"

"She will let you know, for dogs responds best to a soft tone—their hearing is many times more acute than that of humans—and she is already used to yours and you have a gentle voice. But it will not be your voice alone that Honey will respond to. It will be your body language, what you do with your hands, caressing, rebuking, pointing a finger. It will be your facial expression, stern and set, smiling and tender.

And your eyes! You were one of the first to discover the importance of eye contact. Now, stay where you are. I'm going to leave, but only if Honey remembers to tell you to come with me when she hears me say your name."

The trainer went to the door, started to open it, then turned back to call "Willa—"

Willa saw the word on her lips. Honey who was lying down and licking her paws looked up, momentarily uncertain. When she heard the name again she went to Willa, put her head in the outstretched hand, then looked toward the door. She put her paw on Willa's knee, conveying in her way that Willa was wanted. When she and Willa reached the door her reward came in words that charmed her. "Good girl, Honey, oh such a good girl."

"Practice this often while you are here and with your friends at home, for your name is a new word for Honey and it will take time for it to register. Never miss the chance to love, to let Honey know how needed she is and what good work she is doing."

That afternoon the class had a health lesson; with their dogs beside them they went to the kennels to see how a bath was given. The dog used in the demonstration seemed to enjoy every minute of the process. He had recently been given to the program by a couple who had been living in Greece. They had found him lying on the side of a road outside Athens. His throat had been cut and he had been left to die. They took him to the authorities and were told of a veterinarian who bandaged the wound and gave the necessary medication. No owner could be found, so the Americans were given the dog's papers and brought him home with them when they returned. As they could not keep him he was offered to the program. Medium in size, smooth hair, black, with a one-sided smile, Kelly passed the test and endeared himself to everyone.

His training was slowed by the fact that he had to learn a new language. The Americans who rescued him had two small children, so Kelly was matched to go to a home in the Midwest where there were two children, but that would not be for another month as he was in training for the next class. Kelly smiled his twisted smile and shook himself free of water when he was taken from the tub and the lesson was over.

Back in the big room the instructor showed the students how to keep their dogs' ears clean, swabbing them once a week, if necessary, with cotton dipped in an antiseptic lotion; how to check their eyes and their teeth; and how to keep their nails trimmed. They were told of the need for periodic visits to a veterinarian for essential shots—parvo virus, rabies— heart worm tests and medication, and fecal examinations. "We know how to take care of ourselves. Your dogs are part of yourselves—they are your ears, and they deserve the best care you can give them."

Each day there was more to learn, more to experience, as the matched pairs became smoothly functioning teams. They were taken into stores and shopping malls. They went to restaurants, and when the students sat at tables the dogs went under the tables. They were told to sit, then they were given the down-stay command, which would last through the meal. Leashes were rarely relied on, but they were still attached. The public library was accustomed to Seeing Eye Dogs, now Hearing Ear dogs accompanied borrowers. Passing a church, one student looked questioningly at a trainer, who assured her that where she went her dog could go. "But, remember, it will be up to you to see that at all times your dog is obedient to you and that you are aware of your dog."

Always near but deliberately unobtrusive, as the dogs were no longer theirs, the trainers were ever watchful, sizing up the growing relationships, the matching that had been done. They saw points that would be taken up with the different owners. One needed to praise her dog more, another needed to allow more independence within the six-foot range, another more relaxation between commands. Even Honey should be permitted to be a bit of a rascal occasionally. Dogs were one answer to the problem of deafness, but they should not be expected to solve people's personal problems. They were not psychiatrists in fur coats but canines with differing temperaments and inborn tendencies to be developed or sometimes to be corrected.

"Fun and games are as good for dogs as they are for us," the instructor called. "So, to the field for some baseball."

Sides were chosen and everyone available took part. Willa had not held a bat in her hands for years, but luck was with her and she hit hard one of the balls pitched to her. She ran to first base, Honey loping beside her, then to second, then to third and home. Players shouted. Dogs barked. Honey panted. Willa, seeing the excitement, reached down to stroke her dog. Each knew that something big had been accomplished. The game went on and there were other home runs, but Willa's first gave her a tingling of something that had been missing from her life for a long time.

"Play often with your dogs," the instructor was saying as they walked back to the house. "The more faithfully they work for you, the more sure they should be of the sheer joy it is to be with you. Run with them off lead in a park or field, whatever is near for you; throw a ball and let them bring it back so you can throw it again. And do dogs like Frisbees? Well, see for yourselves. It's all good exercise for you both and will keep you in training for the dog show next spring."

"Dog show?"

"Yes, it takes place every year and we hope you'll all come back for it. Competition is keen and there are all kinds of classes—for the Best Groomed, the Most Improved, Special Tricks, Best Tail Wag, and the crown of them all is Superdog. Even if you don't get a prize, it gives you a chance to show off your dog. Many sponsors come to the show and that helps the program."

It was hard to believe that the last day had come, but the students had the comforting feeling that they would keep in touch with each other and with the program. Learning to work with their dogs and relating to them, they had related to each other and felt bonded as if by invisible leashes. Each day that added a stride toward independence marked a deepening of friendship. Willa was not the only one who felt confidence replacing the anxiety that had overshadowed many of her days.

The ceremony that night was as solemn as it was challenging. Each one was given a yellow harness and yellow leash, the right size and length for the particular dog, marked in strong black letters HEARING EAR DOG; each was given an ID card with a picture of the dog and the names of both dog and owner. The card was indication of their graduation. "It is more than identification," the instructor explained, "it is a passport. As you have been told, your dogs are now certified by law to be with you wherever you go."

She held up a small booklet, *Legal Rights of Dog Guides for the Deaf.* "Forty-eight states have written this law into their statutes, and though the wording differs a little it is basically the same," then she read from Chapter 272-98A, "*Massachusetts law guarantees a deaf person the legal right to be accompanied by a specially trained dog in all public accommodations and on all public conveyances* and it says clearly that *no extra charge can be levied because of the presence of the dog guide* and that the user— that's you and you and you—*can be required to produce identification such as the card furnished by the school from which the dog was obtained.* So, keep your IDs always at hand."

A collective smile passed over the group and hands stroked, patted, and embraced their dogs. Tails wagged. Cookie's went fast, others more slowly, Honey's thumped on the floor. Something had happened that pleased her owner and that was all she needed to be pleased. Willa leaned toward her and whispered, "You may win the prize for the Best Tail Wag when it's time for the show." Honey's tail thumped harder.

"There's something more you should know," the instructor went on, "the Internal Revenue Service has decreed that any moneys expended on your dogs for licenses, veterinarian fees, food, are all tax deductible."

Again the collective smile, again the tails wagged and one thumped.

"The card you carry indicates that you as well as your dog have been professionally trained. What you both have is a privilege and that is also a responsibility."

There were some in the group who read the words on the instructor's lips and saw the same in sign language. The word "responsibility" is a hand laid upon the shoulder where a burden is carried; in this case it was a burden proudly, gladly carried. Laws had been made and would be enforced so a certain number of people deprived of hearing could, with their dog guides, move more freely in a hearing world. Seeing the words and the gesture, Willa leaned close to Honey and whispered something into her ear. "Perhaps" was the word. So much had once seemed impossible; so much now seemed possible.

Solemnity tired the dogs and most of them were ready to flatten out in sleep, but it fired the trainers. Relieved that one more class was safely launched, they were eager to reminisce about other dogs that belonged to the program.

"Remember Banjo?" one asked and the others nodded. "He heard the smoke alarm before anyone else and went to arouse his owner and get her to the door, then he went back, crawling along the floor to rouse the other members of the household and get them out."

"And Bowen, remember what he did?"

Bowen, a former sheep dog, had been given to the program when his owner died. Used to herding cattle and sheep, he knew what numbers were in his care and never ceased his rounding until the last one was accounted for. Ten years old and placed in a home for the elderly, he soon learned to respond not to one resident but to everyone in the house. The first time there was a fire drill he went to each room in turn and got its occupant to safety. Nothing deterred him until all were accounted for. The cook, knowing it was just a drill, did not leave the kitchen, but Bowen would not let her stay.

"Remember? She said she wouldn't have had a skirt to her name if she hadn't finally yielded to his tugging."

"Chico was a Superdog, but then he had a college education."

"By association."

Chico was a chihuahua who had been kept secretly by some men in their college dormitory, fed, played with, generally enjoyed. When the year was over, as he didn't belong to anyone in particular, he had been left. A custodian found him sitting all alone on a cot stripped down to a mattress. He looked as if he wondered what would happen next. The custodian took him to the shelter and the shelter offered him to the program. He passed all the tests given him and went into training. Chico was smart and his butterfly ears made him adept for sounds. Matched to a woman who had lost her hearing due to a stroke and was confined to a wheel chair, he spent most of his time in her lap. Light and swift, he would get to a door while the knock was still sounding or to the TTY while it was still ringing, then back and forth until his owner wheeled herself to the source.

"Chico writes good letters. We hear from him two or three times a year."

"Remember Flora?"

"Oh, poor Flora! We found her in a bus station. She had crawled into a corner behind some boxes and had just given birth to three tiny puppies. Two were already dead, one had a slim chance at life and it was saved. Flora was so thin, her ribs almost stuck through her skin. She was so mangy and dirty you could hardly see what kind of dog she was. We brought her to the shelter where she was cleaned up and could nurse her one pup, then to the vet. She was fed, bathed, cared for, and in a month she could have won a beauty contest. She had all the markings of a collie but she was short haired. She responded to training as if she had been born to guide, and within a year she entered a new life as a certified Hearing Ear Dog. She went to California. Who knows, she may be headed for Hollywood and a new career."

"Look at Ebony now."

"And remember then. Found wandering in a parking lot. When an owner was located he said he didn't want him and had turned him loose. Maybe someone would put him to sleep, but he didn't have the money for that. We took him."

"And Jack?"

"Oh, that's hard to believe. His people moved away, neighbors saw the van and all the furniture loaded into it, the blinds in the house go down, and the FOR SALE sign go up. Next day they found Jack tied to a tree in the backyard. He was taken to the shelter and the owners were traced. Their reply was that they thought someone might want him, they didn't."

Willa drew her hand across Honey's smooth head and looked into the eyes that returned her gaze. She didn't want to know about Honey's past. It was the present that mattered. Like the others she had been given a purpose in life, work to do that needed doing and for which she had been trained. After a few moments, Willa lifted her head. They were talking about Molly, the little dog she had seen on TV the night her life took a new direction.

"Molly may be small in size, but she does everything the others do and she has a special way that is all her own. You'll discover this with your dogs. They'll all develop something you've never taught them, and their company will give you added pleasure. Molly goes with one of us as a demonstration dog when we give talks to inform people about the program. After our work has been shown and explained I say, 'If anyone would like to contribute a dollar or more, Molly will be glad to take it.'

"Someone is bound to respond, drawing a bill from purse or wallet and waving it in the direction of Molly. She trots to the person, accepts it in her teeth, and trots right back to me with it, then she looks expectantly around the room. One person after another wants to test her and she is kept busy. The denomination doesn't matter, its the crinkly sound that attracts her—perhaps its shape or color—and she is never fooled. You'll meet her next spring when you come back for the dog show and picnic."

It was getting late, but the instructor had one more thought to leave with the graduates. "Just realize that a dog's life span is shorter than a human's. It may be that in time you will return for another dog. There will be one for you—one who needs your love and who has learned to give as you have to receive."

Later in her room, yellow harness and leash hanging over a chair and Honey chewing on a rawhide bone, Willa read the final sheet of instructions that had been given out. Even though she was no longer student but graduate, she knew that education was a continuing affair and that it would be up to her to keep both Honey and herself in training by reintroducing the sounds and bringing new ones into use. It would be work, for Honey was a working dog, but it could be done as a game, too, and there would always be the reward in more than words. Should a friend be visiting and want to answer any sound, Honey was the trained one and should not be deprived of her right to work. Privilege—responsibility—the words were interchangeable, but one belonged more specifically to Honey, the other to Willa.

The following morning the dogs were taken for brisk walks to make sure elimination was complete before their journeys began in plane or bus or private car. Two proud owners were being called for by friends; two went off in the airport limousine; one had her own car and took the wheel with new confidence because of the copilot beside her.

The instructor and trainers stood on the steps of the building and watched them go. "Keep in touch. Write or phone if any problem arises, and know that the outreach worker is always available for a visit. Keep the bonding of your leashes for another few days. The dogs will be in strange surroundings and they will need to gain confidence from you. Good-bye, good-bye."

Willa sat in the bus as she had two weeks ago, but now there was someone curled at her feet, and in her hand was a yellow leash attached to a collar and a harness with words that would be honored wherever she went. Honey was giving her companionship and with it independence; what she gave in return was love. She reached down to stroke the golden head and a warm tongue drew itself across her hand. Who needed to hear any words?

Two

🐾   🐾

IT WAS MID-AFTERNOON when Willa turned the key in the lock and let herself and Honey into the apartment. The rooms had the reproachful air of having been closed too long, and Willa went through them opening windows, then she picked up the mail on the floor that had come through the slot in the door. There were bills to pay, letters to answer, reminding her of people she must call on to let them know she was back. It would be easier to make calls now that Honey was with her. She checked the refrigerator to see what was needed. At the same time she introduced the apartment to Honey. By her bed she spread Honey's blanket on the floor, and while Willa was unpacking Honey made herself into a circle and settled on it.

"Not yet, Honey, there's much more to show you." Willa startled herself with the realization that she now had someone to talk to. "And talk to your dogs often," she could hear the instructor saying. "It's good for both of you. It doesn't matter that one of you doesn't hear and the other doesn't speak, it keeps avenues of communication open."

In the kitchen Willa filled a bowl with water that Honey sniffed, then knowing that it was for her lapped delightedly. From the kitchen, the door of the little backyard opened and they went out for Honey to discover the area where she would be free of the leash. She made the rounds then returned to Willa and the comfort of her presence in a world where everything was new. Willa showed her the front door where a knock would be a summons, then they returned to the bedroom and Willa showed Honey the alarm clock that would be another summons.

Fully as important as the surroundings was getting to know each other. At the training center they had taken each other for granted; it might be different here. Willa sat down in a low chair and called Honey to a position between her knees so she could look into her eyes.

"You are Honey," she said slowly. "Honey. Honey."

At the sound of her name Honey quivered and started to rise, expectant of a command.

Willa pushed her down, then pointed to herself. "Willa." She repeated the name. Still pointing to herself she said, "Miss Macy. Sometimes, Honey, that is what you will hear people say, and both names mean me."

She left Honey and went across the room. Honey's eyes followed her. "Honey, come to Willa." Honey bounded across the room to stand beside her. She was rewarded with a warm "Good girl," then told to stay while Willa left her to recross the room. Bending low and clapping her hands, Willa said, "Honey, come to Miss Macy," and Honey did. The reward then was more than words, it was an embrace. Willa was pleased at Honey's response but knew that it was something they would have to work on constantly. There would be times, at the office especially, when Honey would need to answer to the more formal name.

Willa looked earnestly at Honey and said, "Wait, now, I'll be back," then left her to go to the nearby convenience store to do what shopping was needed. When she returned Honey almost knocked her over in welcome.

"You'll have to get used to my leaving you sometimes, but

on Monday we'll go to the office together. No more work today, Honey, let's just enjoy each other."

On Sunday afternoon Willa let the kettle in the kitchen boil longer than she usually did. Honey heard it. Looking up from a careful licking of her paws she ran to the kitchen, realized the situation and raced back to tell Willa. "Good girl," was her commendation, "thank you, Honey." Willa turned the stove off, made herself a cup of tea and prepared Honey's supper. "Someday, Honey, we may have a TTY, then you can tell me when to answer the phone, but they are very expensive. We'll have to wait."

Monday morning the alarm went off at six o'clock. Long before it ceased ringing, Honey's paws were on the bed and her nose was nuzzling Willa; then her long tongue began licking Willa's cheeks.

"That's enough," Willa said, stroking her, not sure whether to laugh or cry at Honey's enthusiasm.

Honey, knowing she had accomplished her duty, went to the back door and put her nose to the crack. Willa let her out then went to shower and dress. By the time they were both ready for the day, breakfast was at hand—a bowl of cottage cheese and a biscuit for Honey, while Willa sat at the table with coffee and toast. "Was the coffee all that bad at the training center?" she asked herself, for never had coffee tasted so good.

It was only a few blocks to the Locke Insurance Company and Willa generally walked, but this time she took the bus. "Use the privilege that is yours," she could hear the instructor saying, "and remember, you're pioneers in this field."

Standing at the bus stop, pocketbook in right hand, Honey's leash in left, she watched as the big gray bus came around a corner and drew to a stop. The door opened partially and the driver leaned toward her. "It's nice to see you back, Miss Macy, but dogs aren't allowed on. Sorry."

Willa held Honey's leash toward him with the words HEAR-ING EAR DOG clearly marked in black letters on the broad yellow band. "This dog is," she said. She reached into her purse for her ID card which she had been taught to have ready when needed.

The driver glanced at it, looked puzzled, then smiled and opened the door its full width. "This is a first for me, and the company too. It's something to have a first on a Monday morning. Should mean good luck for the week."

What he said meant no more to Willa than it did to Honey; what mattered was that the steps could be mounted and there was a seat near the door.

Willa was known to be an early arrivee at the office, but others were there before her. Several of the staff standing near the door made themselves a welcoming committee. Hands reached out, first to grasp Willa's then to stroke Honey's head.

"Isn't she beautiful!"

"Aren't you lucky!"

"First dog ever to be in the office!"

The remarks passed over Willa like a spring breeze, but the smiles gave her the assurance of acceptance; and on her desk was a vase of flowers and a dog biscuit tied with a pink ribbon.

One of the men stood before her and said, "When you are settled, Mr. Locke would like to see you and your friend."

Willa nodded. "We'll go momentarily." She took only long enough to put her purse away and gather up notebook and pencil.

Mr. Locke rose and held out his hand to her. "You've been missed, but there wasn't a person in the office who was not delighted at what you were doing, and they have all had a part in it."

Honey, standing beside Willa, was composed but attentive, and when Mr. Locke looked down at her she solemnly lifted her right front paw and placed it against his leg.

"Well mannered, isn't she?" he commented.

"More than that." There was much Willa wanted to say,

but it was Monday morning. She had been away a month and there was work to be done.

"These reports, Miss Macy, are ready to be typed. I'll be glad to have them before you leave this afternoon." He faced her directly, spoke clearly and slowly as he went over them.

"You shall," she replied, "my fingers are itching to get back to the keys." She took the papers in her right hand, gave Honey a command, a pull on the leash and they were out the door.

"Oh, Miss Macy, just one thing more—" Mr. Locke stopped, realizing he was talking to a disappearing back. He turned to his desk. Why was it so hard to remember that she did not get words directed to her unless she was face to face? He looked up to see her standing beside his desk.

"Honey brought me back. You have something more for me?"

"Yes, I—I—" Mr. Locke was puzzled. "How was it you heard me call you?"

"I didn't. Honey blocked my way. She wouldn't go forward until I turned and came back to your office."

"Smart dog, beginning to show the worth of our investment. Yes, Miss Macy, I have another letter, a personal one. I'd like you to do it today. Take it down now, if you please."

Willa's notebook and pencil were ready. She was used to Mr. Locke's dictation, used to keeping her eye on his lips and trusting shorthand to her fingers.

"Denis Talcot, 64 Sycamore Street," she read back to Mr. Locke, "I am glad to second your application for custodial work at St. Martin's. You have already received your instructions and a check will be mailed to you the first of every month."

Mr. Locke listened while Willa read, then he nodded, but he seemed inclined to talk. "He's a nice young fellow, getting his Masters in Social Work, wants to do something with juvenile delinquents. In my day we called them bad boys." Mr. Locke looked away and Willa did not get all of what he was saying, but comments had nothing to do with the content of the letter.

"I'll do it now, Mr. Locke, and bring it back to you for signing when I have the reports ready." She closed her notebook, gave Honey a signal, and the two left the room.

At lunch time Willa took Honey out for a brief walk. Returning, she tied her to her desk and went to the cafeteria. People crowded around her, asking questions.

"Can Honey roll over if you tell her to?"

"Why?"

"Show how clever she is."

"She'll show that in other ways. Honey is a working dog."

"Will she sit up if I give her some dog candy?"

"Honey doesn't beg for treats, but she is rewarded by them for special behavior."

"Doesn't she do any tricks?"

"She'll do what she's trained to do, alert me to certain sounds. A Hearing Ear Dog doesn't do tricks. You'll see."

What they did see, and it happened several times during the day, was that when someone approached Willa from the side or from behind, she turned to face the person and was often the first to begin a conversation. Honey had given her a cue.

The office closed at four. Willa walked home, knowing she had just time enough to go by the Town Hall and secure a dog license for Honey. She put on the clerk's desk the ID she and Honey shared and Honey's vaccination certificate. She was prepared to explain her request, but the clerk was ready for her.

"Mr. Locke told me you'd be in and I've set aside a special license for your dog. Now, give me her name, breed, age, and I'll clip the license on to her collar. She's one in a hundred, you know."

"I do know. Her name is Honey, she is a golden retriever, spayed female, three years old." Willa looked at the license, shaped like a little bone: the number on it was One. She smiled, realizing they were both being given something to live up to.

Honey did not seem impressed by her distinction, but she relished the fondling the clerk gave her.

"Likes affection, doesn't she?"

"It's her life." Willa opened her purse to pay the fee.

The clerk shook her head. "Seeing Eye Dogs and Hearing Ear Dogs pay no fee. The town is honored by their presence, and Honey is the first of her kind here as well as being Number One."

Willa thanked the clerk and Honey offered her right paw, then they went on their way.

Returning from the cafeteria on Wednesday, Willa discovered one of the staff on the floor beside Honey feeding her half a hamburger which Honey was devouring with gusto.

"I want her to like me," was the explanation, "and she did look so hungry."

"Honey has her own food," Willa said, "and she eats at her own times. Giving a dog tidbits is not the way to win affection. Your hands stroking her will tell her you love her. If she offers you her paw, accept it. That's her evidence of friendship."

One of the young pages came up to Willa, hand in his pocket. Honey looked at him, then put her head down between her paws and simulated sleep.

"What kind of a dog is that, anyway? I've been buzzing this thing until it's nearly worn out and all she does is look at me."

"Let Honey see you put it on my desk and set it to go off in a few minutes, then go back to your work, but be sure she sees you."

Five minutes later the buzzer went off with a sound far more strident than when it was pocketed. Honey stood up, looked at it, put a paw on Willa's knee, looked at Willa then at the boy who was standing near a file cabinet. Willa picked up the gadget and went to the boy with it.

"See? She alerted me to the sound, which is what she is

supposed to do, then she looked from me to you because she saw you put it on my desk and connected you with the sound."

The boy's teasing expression was washed out by admiration. "She really does think, doesn't she! What do I do now?"

"Tell her she's a good girl, love her, let her know you're friends."

Even though Willa had been outspoken about Honey's diet, there were still some who could not resist feeding her with morsels from their lunches. A paper cup of coleslaw was offered to Honey; partly because she was polite and partly because she could not resist attention she ate it. It was not long before she went over to a corner of the room and relieved herself of it. Returning to her place beside Willa, Willa thought she saw a slightly smug look about Honey as if she could be relied on to handle things in her own way.

Willa had not heard the retching sounds but her nose told her all she needed to know. She saw what had happened and cleaned it up as quickly as possible, glad that she could not hear the comments that were being made. When she returned from the washroom, Mrs. Golding went up to her and said, "If that dog is so smart she should know what doesn't agree with her and refuse it."

Willa reached down to stroke Honey. "With dogs we do what is possible within a certain range. Honey has had only intermediate training. If she had gone on for advanced, that is one of the lessons she would be taught—to refuse any food except that from the hand of her owner."

Mrs. Golding was determined to have the last word. "I'm going to speak to Mr. Locke about having a dog in a business office. Some of us have allergies to animal hair."

On Friday afternoon when Willa delivered some reports to Mr. Locke, he asked how people were taking to the presence of a dog.

"Some people understand dogs more than others."

"It's up to you, of course, to see that Honey is under control at all times."

"Two words were made very clear to us, Mr. Locke, when we were in training—privilege and responsibility. Neither Honey nor I will let the program down, or betray your confidence in us."

"It's always 'we' isn't it?"

"Yes, of course, Honey and I are a team."

Willa went back to her desk to cover her typewriter and put some papers away. The others had gone. It was not unusual, she was often the last person to leave. Honey looked at her intently then raced out to the hallway and to the door of the Ladies Room, back to Willa, then back again to the door.

"Honey, that's not the way we go out. Come," she picked up the leash and went toward the front door, but Honey had no intention of going that way. To humor her, Willa went toward the Ladies Room, then she saw that one of the doors was being beaten on so that it was shaking. Obviously someone was knocking. Willa put her hand on Honey's head. "Someone's trying to get out. Why didn't I trust you! We're here," she called. "I'll see if I can loosen the lock from the outside, it's always been tricky."

Working with the aid of a nail file, Willa finally eased the lock and out plunged Mrs. Golding. Her face was streaked with tears, distorted by panic.

"Honey heard you knocking. That's one of her sounds." Willa tried to calm the distraught lady. "She thought you wanted to get in but it was out."

"Why, I might have been here all weekend," Mrs. Golding half sobbed, still trembling, then she looked at Honey and suddenly dropped to her knees putting her arms around the dog. "You blessed animal," she said. She looked up at Willa, "What did you say her name was?"

"Honey."

"She's that all right. Can't I give her something to show her how grateful I am?"

"Your love is doing that."

"The door—what happened?"

"It looks as if the bolt got jammed. I'll leave a note for the janitor to fix it when he comes in Monday morning."

Willa did not set the alarm for Saturday morning, but she woke up not far from her usual time. She glanced across the room to the corner where Honey had her nest. Curled up into a round ball, she was sleeping soundly. Willa luxuriated in a long slow stretch and the realization that she did not have to get up at a prescribed time. They had both been tired and had earned the right to sleep in. Willa was always in a state of tension at work, having to be ready to give "ear" to whomever came to her desk and make an effort not to be startled. This week it had been easier as Honey invariably nudged her knee at the sound of approaching footsteps. Willa could look up and be ready to face friend or colleague. Alerted, it was possible to smile, knowing that someone was coming to her for something she could do.

Honey had been attentive every day and this morning she had good reason to relax. Willa snuggled into the bed clothes and went back over the week. Honey had done well enough for her to send a good report back to the program. That first occasion when she had responded to "Miss Macy" and returned her to Mr. Locke proved something to him. Honey was alert; and last night's experience in the Ladies Room spoke for itself. Honey began to stir, uncurling herself, rising and stretching slowly, shaking herself and stretching again, then she looked across the room. Willa's eyes were open and gazing at her; then it was as if Honey suddenly realized there was work to do. She leaped across the room and started licking Willa's face, stopping only long enough to peer at the alarm clock on the table.

"It's all right, Honey, this is the day we have to ourselves."

The yellow harness and leash remained on a rack near the door. After breakfast Willa went to her desk to catch up with long neglected mail and Honey went back to her nest. "That's right, Honey, when there's nothing else to do, rest. We never know when something might call us into action again."

After an hour Willa was prompted to go to the bedroom and there she saw Honey working away methodically at a project of her own. She had very nearly removed the zipper from the outer cover of the pillow that was her nest. "Honey, what are you doing!" Willa exclaimed.

Honey looked up, wagged her tail and went back to her zipper.

"No, no, you mustn't do that." The words rose in Willa but she did not utter them.

For reasons known only to Honey the zipper was being removed from the outer covering, the inner pillow that held cedar shavings was intact, stoutly sewed, and seemed to hold no interest. Willa told herself she would get another zipper, or perhaps replace it with buttons. Honey, so used to working, probably had to find something to do and a little tooth testing had appealed to her. Words of one of the trainers echoed in Willa, "Every dog has to be a bit of a rascal now and then."

After a while Willa said "That's enough," in a tone that was anything but stern. Honey left the tangled threads, the length of zipper, and went to stand beside her, looking up into her face, licking her hand; everything in her ready to respond.

Later on they had a practice session and Willa ran through some of the sounds to which Honey had been trained to respond—not the door knock, which had already been well tried, but the timer in the kitchen, the tea kettle, and the smoke alarm that could be activated by holding a flashlight close to it. Honey went through them all, dutifully but not enthusiastically, as if she knew they were not for real.

Willa, always looking for ways to extend her range, left a water tap running in the cellar while Honey was out in the yard. Honey paid no attention until she settled into her nest for a second sleep and Willa started to lose herself in a book. Watching surreptitiously, she saw Honey lift her head, cock it, then go to the door that led down to the cellar. Honey stayed beside it but did not nose it open to go down and investigate. After a few moments of obvious uncertainty over a sound new to her, she went to Willa and put her paw on her knee to get attention. Once gained, she went back to the cellar door and waited. Willa responded to the signal and went down cellar to turn off the dripping tap. When she returned she embraced Honey. "Good girl," she said over and over. Dripping water was one more sound she could add to Honey's list.

The letters on her desk told Willa of things she should do, people she should see, but she deferred answering them. The week at the office had given her and Honey all the new experiences and people they needed and more could wait. Ever since she had been deaf, Willa's tendency had been to withdraw, to retreat into herself. It was an effort to be with people, to converse in the only way she could by watching lips and then replying as best she could. Often the effort drained her of energy that should have gone into sociability. Today, this weekend, was for Honey and herself, but it was too nice a day to stay indoors. She called to Honey, fitted the yellow harness on her, and fastened the leash to her collar. Together they went to the nearby park for a walk.

There where the grass was green she gave Honey her freedom, but Honey took it warily and soon returned to Willa for the assurance of the leash and her company. A few people spoke to Willa, attracted by Honey whose friendliness was evident. Seeing the words HEARING EAR DOG, they asked questions. Willa found her desire to withdraw diminishing when she could talk about Honey.

On the way home she passed St. Martin's and saw someone raking leaves. "Nice young fellow," Mr. Locke's words recurred to her. Willa had imagined someone not much more than a boy, but this was a tall man, raking as if he knew what he was about and with a vigor that implied there must be no leaf left on the lawn when Sunday morning came. A young woman emerged from the church and went up to him. The rake was put down and the two talked together, even laughed. Willa saw it all without turning her head, she had become adept at using the corners of her eyes. She quickened her pace. Honey, loving people and jollity, gave a little pull at the leash as much as to say "Why don't we join them?" Willa drew the leash in tightly, said "Honey, heel," in a firm tone and at the next intersection turned down the street that would take her home and away from St. Martin's.

Pictures lingered in her mind long after she got back to her apartment, long after she had given Honey her daily grooming, long after she had had supper and settled down to read a book. She kept seeing the busy young man, joined by the pretty young woman, the way he had put down his rake to talk with her, the way she had said something to make him laugh. What had they been talking about? What were they laughing about? Had he gone back to leaf raking or gone into the church with her? Then loneliness closed in around Willa like a wall. It was an old feeling, she knew it well, so well that she had learned to accept it. It would go after awhile like a pain, but this time it did not go. She put her head in her hands and started to cry. Tears came in a flood and wracking sobs shook her shoulders.

The sobs were audible to Honey, who went to Willa's side as readily as if she had been called. She waited patiently, but there was no response. Honey's soft warm tongue began lapping the hands, then the cheeks as they were uncovered, then she looked at Willa.

"Nobody taught you the sound of a sob," Willa said, when she felt herself in control, "but now you know. Now you know."

During the next few weeks Honey was acknowledged to be a full-fledged member of the office staff. She sat most of the time by Willa's desk, but there were moments when she made brief visits to others, especially to Mrs. Golding whose fondling was always lavish and who made no mention of any allergy. Honey's retriever instinct was in evidence when wastepaper aimed at a basket missed its mark. She would rise quietly, pick it up and return it to the sender, standing with her tail wagging and an expectant look. Everyone knew now that the look asked for a show of affection and it was readily given.

It had been impressed on Willa at the training center that a Hearing Ear Dog owner had the opportunity to make such dogs and their work known. Willa's long-time reluctance to face strangers was being overcome because of Honey, and for the sake of other Honeys and the people who needed them she braved new encounters. One such was the Post Office which had a sign on its door saying NO DOGS ALLOWED EXCEPT SEEING EYE DOGS. Mustering her courage one Saturday morning, she went in with Honey and asked to see the postmaster.

Ushered into his office she placed herself opposite him where the light was on his face. She introduced Honey, displaying the harness and leash with their descriptive words, showed her ID, and requested that the sign on the door include Hearing Ear Dogs. The postmaster started to demur but Honey, as if on cue, put her right paw on his knee and looked at him with eyes that he later said could melt a stone.

"Are there any other such dogs in town, Miss Macy?"

"Not yet, but there are two people who need them."

The postmaster asked more about the program and Willa found herself doing what had never been easy for her to do —talking with someone she scarcely knew.

"We'll take care of that sign, and soon," were the final words, as the postmaster stroked Honey's head.

Willa left, cheered by the feeling that one mission had been accomplished.

She repeated the process at the bank and at the library, but they were places where she was known and recognition made it easier. The supermarket should be next on her list, but she dreaded the confrontation. Her shopping had always been done at the convenience store near her apartment where she was well known. A time for the supermarket came sooner than she expected. At the end of the first month when pay checks were delivered, Willa was surprised to see two envelopes on her desk, one with Honey's name on it. She opened to read that it was a certificate for $25 to purchase Honey's favorite food at the Sunnyside Supermarket.

"Oh, but I've never gone there!" Willa exclaimed.

The office staff congratulated Honey while Willa had misgivings. The store was so big, often crowded, and she knew none of the clerks. Willa shook her head with uncertainty.

Mrs. Golding spoke up brightly, "I'm going there tonight on my way home. Let's go together."

Willa smiled, the rare smile that said more than words. She was touched that people wanted to help her. Perhaps people would always have been willing, but she had held them at bay. Embarrassment, timidity, diffidence had driven her deep into herself, but she was beginning to shake such feelings off the way Honey shook rain from her coat when she came in out of the wet. "Thank you," she murmured.

It was not easy in the supermarket. Many people looked askance at Willa, and there were obviously those who felt that a place where food was sold was no place for a dog. Willa kept her ID in one hand, leash in the other, and Honey trotted beside the cart that was rapidly filling. Mrs. Golding, walking beside them with her own cart, was ready to do battle if needed or extol something so remarkable as a dog who heard for its owner who could not hear.

That night when Willa was putting her purchases away in the kitchen with Honey watching intently, she looked as directly at Honey as she liked to have people look at her. "Honey, you are giving me confidence. I'm doing things I've shied away from, dreaded doing, for years and years. Thank you!"

It was not the words so much as the embrace that made Honey wag her tail.

Assurance was coming to Willa in many ways, through many avenues, but it toppled late one night. She was reading, curled up on the couch with Honey at her feet. Honey stirred and stood up, glanced around the room then went to the window that looked out on the backyard. Returning to Willa, she nuzzled her then went back to the window, nosing it intently. Willa felt a runnel of fear through her. This was something she had been advised about during training. The dogs were schooled to warn of any unusual sound, even a possible intruder.

The window was closed, the shade was down, no one could see in but could anyone get in? Willa spoke sternly to Honey, pointed to her place on the floor and told her to lie down; but Honey would not leave the window. Finally Willa yielded. Approaching the window, she said in a firm voice "Who's there?" and ran the shade up. She started at what she saw: a shutter had come loose and was banging against the window frame. She had felt weak with fear, now she felt weak with relief and wanted only to sit down on the floor and laugh at herself, but she knew Honey would give her no peace until the noise was stopped.

Willa ran the window up, pushed the shutter back on the hook from which it had become loosened. Then she sat down on the floor and hugged Honey. "Thank you," she said, "that's another one of your sounds, isn't it?"

Their approach to the park for the usual Saturday morning romp took them close to St. Martin's. Willa was careful to walk on the sidewalk across the street from the church, but she had not seen the "nice young fellow" again.

Perhaps, leaves having all fallen, he was working inside the church. She was torn between wanting to see him and fearful as to what she would say if they ever did meet. Honey was often the one to make the introduction, but Willa did not feel easy about this meeting. She had an advantage in that she knew his name. If they did meet, she would have to tell him hers, then point to the words on Honey's leash. Safely past St. Martin's without an encounter, she met a little girl in the park who was tossing a Frisbee into the air and racing gleefully after it.

Spying the dog, the child ran up to Willa. "What's your dog's name?"

"Honey."

"Does she like to play Frisbee?"

"I don't know." Willa looked at Honey who was nosing the disc, tail wagging and tongue alternately licking the little girl's hand and the Frisbee. Honey looked at Willa. Pleading was in her eyes, her stance, her whole being. "Try her." Willa unhooked the leash.

The red disc was tossed into the air. It went high but not far. Honey ran fast, then leaped to catch it. She danced about with it in her mouth and returned it to Willa, so Willa threw it. It went higher, but not too high for Honey to catch it, wheel herself about and return it again to Willa.

"She knows she belongs to you, doesn't she?" the little girl asked, kneeling on the ground with her arms around Honey, her eyes on Willa. "Why didn't you answer me when I called to you the first time Honey caught it?"

"Because I did not hear you. I have to see your lips making words. My ears don't tell me things, but my eyes do." She pointed to the words on the leash. "Honey is my ears."

The child's eyes widened. "Words on lips?" She looked closely at Willa as if she might see words taking actual shape when Willa spoke. "Words," the girl repeated with new respect. Always before, spoken words had been like fluff from a dandelion that disappeared in the distance or released balloons that were soon lost to sight, but they were shapes that could be seen by some people.

"Will you tell me about the words you see when my lips are moving? My name is Rosey," she spoke slowly, wondering what it looked like on her lips.

"And my name is Willa."

Rosey heard but could not see the word, just a mouth opening, lips moving.

Sensing her dismay, Willa smiled comfortingly. "It doesn't happen all at once. People have to study hard to learn speech reading, and some of it is guess work."

"Tell me more. This is like a story."

There was a bench near, so they went over and sat on it. Honey nestled at Willa's feet, settling the golden head on her knee, restful but alert.

It had been a long time since Willa had thought about storytelling, but she remembered what it had meant to her as a little girl when her father had answered her demand for a story, so she told Rosey about the work that Honey did and that there were other dogs training to be ears for deaf people. She showed Rosey some simple signing—the hand on the shoulder that meant burden, the arms lifted high that meant elation. The hand closed but for one finger held against the chest that meant "I," then the hand with one finger pointing outward that meant "You."

Rosey was fascinated. "This is fun," she said, shaping her lips carefully, moving her hands suggestively. "Using more of me makes talk more interesting."

Willa nodded, recalling that the instructor had taught them about using body language with their dogs—the eyes, the facial expression, the finger pointing, the hand widespread in command, curved in caress.

"How do you sign love?"

Willa showed her, arms crossing chest, hands just below the shoulders. "It's so simple, almost the way it feels."

"Is there a book in the library that could tell me about this kind of talking?"

"Many books."

Rosey's face brightened. "Maybe next time we meet I'll have some words for you."

Soon they parted, Rosey picked up her Frisbee and skipping off, Willa and Honey walking on their way. Suddenly Honey stopped short and looked toward the child who was calling back to them. Willa turned and waited. Rosey came running up, her face filled with contrition.

"I'm sorry, I forgot. I just wanted to tell you that I'm going to the library on my way home to get one of those books."

Willa had an almost uncontrollable desire to put her arms around Rosey and hug her, but she had been locked within herself too long to be easily demonstrative with anyone but Honey. Rosey had no such inhibition. She flung her arms around Willa's waist. "This has been the bestest day ever," she paused, then signed "I love you" and raced off across the grass.

"You are making things happen, Honey." At the sound of the familiar voice now directed to her, Honey drew her tongue across the back of Willa's hand. Willa felt so buoyed that she walked right past St. Martin's without troubling to cross to the other side of street.

Willa was ready to admit that during their three months together she and Honey had learned more about each other than they had during the two weeks at the training center. New sounds had been mastered, new ploys discovered, even new games. Willa had begun to be ready for the unexpected, but not for Honey's disappearance.

Three

OPENING THE KITCHEN DOOR one Saturday morning
to call Honey in from her usual time in the yard, no Honey
came. Willa called more insistently, went out and looked all
around the small space, then saw to her dismay that a gate
near the house had been left open and Honey had evidently
walked through it and out into the world. In an agonizing
moment of time Willa thought of the possibilities. Stolen? No.
No one would take a dog clearly identified as having been
trained for a distinct purpose. Curiosity? Normal in an animal.
Adventure? It was built into Honey; but nothing made sense.
Thinking of her breed, her training, her bonding with her
owner, it was unlikely that Honey would sally far on her own.
Yet at the training center they had been told that this might
happen for a variety of reasons. A dog could be as subject to
boredom as a human and act on its own initiative.

Willa knew what she should do: let the police know, alert
the neighborhood, but without a telephone that meant making
personal calls, which she dreaded doing, and she was not
ready for the day. Saturdays moved at a different pace than
other days and she had not dressed yet, but there was no time
to lose. Forego her shower, forego her breakfast, pull on jeans
and a T-shirt and get out. "Honey," she said, as if to test her

voice, knowing that calling would do little good as her voice had such a limited range. Anxiety turned to anguish and got into her fingers, causing them to fumble as she tied the laces on her shoes and one lace after another knotted.

What if Honey had been stolen, picked up by a car that was now miles away to nowhere? What if she had been hit and was lying on the road dead or, worse, had been injured and wandered off to suffer and die as animals did? What if she was kidnapped and was being held for a ransom, tied in some dark and lonely shed? Would she cry pitifully or bark impatiently? Willa was not one to know. All that could happen flashed through her mind as her fingers struggled to loosen the knots and finally tie her shoes. Yet beyond everything was Honey's sweetness. Wouldn't that save her from cruel treatment—but not from a speeding car? Anguish gave way to resolve, and Willa knew that whatever had to be done would be for Honey's sake. She put on her coat, picked up Honey's yellow leash, and went to the front door.

Opening it, she was startled to see a young man with Honey beside him.

"Oh!" Willa's mouth was so dry that almost no sound came from it.

"I've been ringing your bell and knocking for the last five minutes. I thought no one was home."

Honey threw herself against Willa whose hands were ruffling her coat, pressing her close to make sure she was real.

"Oh, thank you, thank you," her voice was faint but returning. "If Honey isn't in the house no bell or knock is heard. She is my ears. Where was she?"

"Snuffling in the shrubbery around St. Martin's."

"You're Denis Talcot, aren't you?" Willa asked, as relief about Honey swept away her feeling of awkwardness with strangers.

"Yes, how did you know?"

"Mr. Locke dictated a letter to you a couple of months ago

that I typed. I've seen you working around St. Martin's. Won't you come in?"

Denis held out his hand. "You're Willa Macy."

"How did you know?"

"Everybody in town knows *of* you, but very few people seem to know you."

Honey stood between them, looking from one to the other like a hostess who has at last achieved an introduction she had long been wanting to make; then, her mission accomplished, she raced in circles of abandonment and joy around the room.

Denis followed Willa and sat down in the chair she gestured to where the light would be on his face. "You speak as if you heard me."

"I see you."

"You're reading my lips?"

Willa nodded. "Speech reading it's called, but it's really speech speculation. Only about thirty percent of all words are visible on lips. There's a lot of guess work and it's helped by expression and gestures."

"That's real communication, isn't it, because it involves so much of the person. Words aren't everything."

A smile flooded Willa's face; it was so rare to be understood and so soon.

Honey took herself off to another part of the room and settled down. Conversation moved between Denis and Willa, each knowing something about the other and reaching for more.

Looking toward Honey, Denis asked, "Is it all right, what she's doing?"

Willa turned around to see. Honey had drawn a cushion from the couch, one that had an outer cover held in place by a zipper. Carefully, methodically, she was working her way around the zipper with the clear intent of removing it from the cushion.

Willa laughed. "That's her one misdeed but now I call it her hobby. She's so well trained and naturally polite, she has never chewed or done anything to merit disapproval except this. I've remonstrated with her, pleaded with her, but somehow I haven't been able to scold her. Removing zippers is her thing and I've decided to let her do it. That one is, I think, the last one available to her. I'm careful not to leave any of my clothes that have zippers within her reach."

It was Denis's turn to laugh. "Almost every dog has some idiosyncrasy," he said, then realizing by Willa's expression that the word was a difficult one, he amended it, "some little way. Each to his own." They laughed together. Honey had broken the ice between them, and conversation flowed easily.

An hour later when Denis left they knew enough about each other to provide the basis for a growing friendship. Willa knew that Denis's parents had been divorced when he was ten and from that time on until his college years he had lived a divided life—the week with his mother, the weekend with his father. His dog, Pundit, a collie, was the only thing of which he could be sure, for Pundit went with him always.

"Where is Pundit now?"

"He came to the end of his days last summer," Denis replied, as quietly as if he might be speaking of a sunset that marked the end of a day. "He was sixteen."

"Last summer," Willa repeated, and her heart lurched toward Denis, "just when Honey was coming into my life."

Denis knew about Willa as much as most people in the town did. She was a shy young woman, profoundly deaf. She had been a good student in school, but after the accident that took her hearing she had gone away to special schools for speech reading, as well as formal studies. During those years she had been protected by her parents. Then one had died and a year later the other. All that she had had of the past was the old dog Poppy; all she could give to the future were the secretarial skills she had acquired. Living alone she became more withdrawn.

He told her about his graduate study and why he wanted to work with delinquent juveniles. "Some of us in high school made up a gang and we did things we knew were not right. We didn't know why we did them. It took me a long time to realize that a prank could lead to a tragedy. There was one, it's haunted me all my life. I'd like to tell you . . ." he turned away, his lips still moving.

Willa leaned toward him and put her hands on his cheeks, turning him back to face her so she could see what he was saying. "Please, I want to know what it is you are going to do."

"Work with young people, find out why they choose to go the wrong way, and head them into the right way. Give them a sense of self-worth. What is delinquency anyway? There's a terrible longing behind it, some kind of misunderstanding, some lack of realization of consequences. Pundit did more for me in those years than any person. I could talk to him, and he never answered back. He just looked at me, and I knew I had to find my own answers."

Willa smiled, remembering Mr. Locke's "delinquent juveniles. I'd call them bad boys."

Standing at the door and finding it hard to leave, Denis said, "On the first Monday evening of the month I sort the bundles and boxes of clothes that people bring to St. Martin's for World Service. Some are in beautiful condition, others deserve—" he shrugged, "obliteration is the only decent word. Come over some evening. There just might be an old pair of zippered jeans that Honey could have some fun with."

"Will you let me help?"

"I'd welcome help. It's a lonely job."

Willa watched him as he went down the street. Lonely—it was a word she knew all too well. So he was lonely, too. Perhaps everyone was at times without being able to say it.

She went over to Honey, sleeping soundly beside her finished task. The cushion was without its cover, the zipper lay curled beside it. Honey's eyes opened when Willa stroked her. "You always do such a neat piece of work." Willa picked up the zipper and put it in the waste basket, the cushion she tossed back to the couch, then they went out to the yard to play ball, Willa throwing nimbly and Honey retrieving expertly.

After the game Willa led Honey to the gate, now securely fastened. She took Honey's nose between her hands, looked her in the eyes and shook her head. Freeing one finger she pointed to the gate and said "No," as firmly as she could. "We never go out that way."

It was the pointing finger and the severe look that got through to Honey. Her eyes, so merry and melting, were mournful; her tail, so constantly in motion, drooped.

Willa's frequent reports back to the program conveyed the assurance that she and Honey were doing all right, so the outreach worker deferred her visit. When she came, she looked with approval at the team they made.

"Honey's coat is handsome; that's because of the right food and daily grooming. Any problems?"

"No, not really. We don't practice all the sounds every day, we alternate for the sake of surprise and we've been discovering some new ones. But tell me of Jack and Cookie, Ebony, Laddie, and Emily. How are they?"

As the stories were related of the dogs Willa had known at the training center, even Honey tilted her head at the sound of names that echoed through the air. "You were an unusual class and are all doing well. The class before you had to return a dog."

"Whatever happened?" It was hard for Willa to imagine how a relationship could fall apart after the weeks of training, the bonding.

"It's not without humor." A roguish smile put Willa at ease. "Bosco was one of the best dogs we ever trained, a beagle-cocker mix, which is good when you get the best of both breeds. He passed all his tests, behaved admirably in training, and acted as if his owner was the only person in the world."

"And then?"

"Once in his new home he was the darling of the family, but he answered no bells, he let kettles boil dry, he was oblivious to knocks, all the time making it quite clear that he was not a working dog, he intended to enjoy his life. The family loved him, but a dog who could hear for the master of the house was their need, so back Bosco came. We found a home for him as a Companion Dog and last I heard he was definitely enjoying life."

"And the man who needed him?"

"He came back for another training session and went home with a dog who took work seriously. They are getting on just fine."

Willa thought of Honey and all she did that was almost taken for granted. "They do work, don't they?"

"Twenty-four hours a day, or whenever a sound alerts them. A Hearing Ear Dog is an ambassador for the program, which reminds me that you may soon be approached by clubs and organizations in this area asking you to demonstrate with Honey and tell about the program."

Willa looked startled and shook her head. "Oh, I couldn't. I can't stand up before people and talk. I—I—"

"But you've told me that Honey is making it easier for you to approach people."

"That's one-to-one. I couldn't stand up before a whole roomful. I'd be so nervous I wouldn't have any words."

"Even so, you wouldn't be doing the demonstration. That would be up to Honey."

"Perhaps."

Gently, persuasively, it was explained that this was something Willa should be willing to do for the program so more and more people would know what Hearing Ear Dogs are and what they can do. "The attention will all be on Honey. She won't let you down, and it's up to you not to let the program down."

Willa looked reluctant though she was ready to agree that the reasoning was valid. "I guess I'm the one who has the problem." Then she thought of the zippers. "I do have a question," and she related Honey's interest in removing zippers. "It's the only mischievous thing she's ever done, but why does she have to do it?"

"Perhaps I can give you an answer. Remember at class, when your instructor was telling you all about the backgrounds of the different dogs, where they came from, and how they arrived at the shelters? There wasn't one who had not been through a rugged experience and Honey's was one of the saddest."

Willa shook her head. What she remembered was that she had been so entranced with Honey and their new relationship that she had not had her eyes on the instructor when she was telling the early histories of the dogs. She remembered, too, that she had not wanted to know where Honey had come from. She was so happy that Honey was where she was then and that she was all hers. "I was not paying attention and no one told me."

"I think it explains everything. One of our staff was driving along a country road and noticed a bag in a ditch. It seemed to be moving. She got out of her car to investigate. Looking more closely, she saw that it was a canvas bag with a zippered fastening. The fastening had been worked apart at one end and a puppy head was peering out from it. She picked the bag up, tore it open so the puppy could get some air. There were two others in the bottom of the bag, but the one whose little teeth tore the zipper apart was the only one that survived. It was Honey. Our staff took her right to a vet, but it was a day or two before he was sure she would make it."

Honey, hearing her name, pressed close to Willa whose arms went around her in the warmest embrace she had ever given.

"There seems to be no end to the means people will take to rid themselves of unwanted animals when it could be so simple: a trip to the vet and a request for euthanasia. But that often costs money."

Willa had no words. Pride in Honey and thankfulness that she had managed to live filled her heart and mind.

"When a request comes up for a demonstration you'll need some help. It always takes two. Shall I drive over or do you have someone near who could lend a hand?"

The shy smile that spoke of inner happiness stole over Willa's face. "I think I can get someone to help."

When the outreach worker left it was with high commendation. "You two are a good match. You have a sound relationship. Honey is doing as much for you as you are for her."

Willa was quite accustomed to meeting Rosey with some of her friends. This Saturday morning Rosey brought her teacher to the park and proudly introduced Miss Spencer to "my special friends, Willa and Honey." It was not long before Rosey ran off with Honey to play Frisbee.

With practice they had both become better. Rosey was adept now at hurling the plastic disc. High it whirled, Honey's eyes on it, her whole body quivering with excitement, as she tried to anticipate where it might land, then leaping to catch it and often doing a whirlabout in the air as she brought it down. She played with it for a moment, even tossed it up on her own, ran off with it, then spun around and raced back to Rosey with it in her mouth.

"Give," Rosey said and Honey dropped the disc, all eagerness for it to be thrown again.

Miss Spencer and Willa had been having a game of their own as Miss Spencer asked Willa if she would come to the school the following Wednesday afternoon and show the children what a Hearing Ear Dog could do for the deaf people.

"They know something about handicaps since we have in the class a legally blind child, who with her braille books and some special teaching, keeps up well with the others. They help her in many ways. To have you and Honey would extend their understanding."

Willa was glad to have people know what Honey could do, and before she had a chance to think what such a visit might mean for her and say "No," she had said "Yes" and set a time for their visit to the school. Mr. Locke had told her more than once that she would be welcome to a few hours off occasionally when there was an opportunity to present Honey and her skills to others. As a sponsor of the program, he felt it was in everyone's interest to have the work of Hearing Ear Dogs widely known.

Breathless and panting from their game, Rosey and Honey returned to hear the news. Impulsively Rosey threw her arms around Willa and gave her a big hug, then she did the same for Honey. "And I'll be your interpreter," she said gleefully, "if you need one."

"The children will ask you questions," Miss Spencer warned, "and they can be very frank in what they want to know."

"I'll try to be ready for them."

When Willa got home, with the rest of the day before her and all the odd tasks that a Saturday presented, she began to have misgivings. What had she gotten herself in for! But it was too late to change her mind and she could not disappoint Rosey.

At the agreed upon time, Willa presented herself at the school. Rosey and a committee of three had been appointed to greet her and lead her to the fourth-grade classroom. A WELCOME sign had been hung on Miss Spencer's desk, and a bowl of water for Honey had been placed on the floor. It was Rosey's honor to introduce her friends, and in doing so she said that Honey would not answer to all the sounds she knew, but that she would to some.

Miss Spencer gave Willa a timer and asked her to set it for the amount of time she would need for the demonstration, after which there would be questions. Willa set it for ten minutes. A boy in the front row stood up. "If she is deaf, how will she hear our questions?"

Rosey had her answer ready. "Look right at Miss Macy, speak clearly and not loudly. She will read your lips."

Willa returned the timer to Miss Spencer and, with Honey close to her left knee, she faced the class and told them the first step in all training was basic obedience. Honey was cooperative in doing the commands with which she was familiar. "Heel." "Sit." "Down." "Come." Each one was accompanied by a hand signal. Sensing the occasion, she performed in a lively way, sometimes anticipating a command before Willa gave it. No one noticed during the exercises that Miss Spencer had slipped out of the room and closed the door behind her. Willa described the different sounds and the way Honey alerted her to them; then there was a loud knocking on the door.

Honey ran to the door, back to Willa, then to the door again. Willa, following her, opened the door and in walked Miss Spencer. The children cheered and clapped their hands. A moment later the timer on the desk went off. Honey faced the sound, nudged Willa's knee, then looked earnestly at her. She raced to the desk, cocked her head at the timer that was still buzzing, and ran back to Willa who was still standing by the door with Miss Spencer. Honey was ready to run back and forth until Willa got the message, went to the desk, picked up the timer and turned it off. Willa faced the class.

"With these two sounds you can see the way she gets my attention, demands my attention really." She leaned toward Honey and embraced her. "Thank you, Honey, you're a good girl. Now lie down and rest for a while." Honey would have preferred to keep performing, but there was a tone and a gesture to which she was bound to comply.

Then came the questions.

"Is it harder to be deaf than to be blind?"

Willa lifted her shoulders and held out her hands. "Who can say? Blindness brings out kindness from people, deafness tends to make people annoyed. They talk louder. That does no good and makes it harder for the lip reader. People can imagine being blind by closing their eyes and keeping them closed. It is not easy for a hearing person to shut out all sound and imagine being deaf. A blind person may wear dark glasses or carry a white cane; deafness is invisible. It has no identification except for those who can benefit from a hearing aid."

She leaned over to pick up Honey's leash and held it so all could see the words HEARING EAR DOG. "Now, when people see me with Honey they know why I have not answered when they call to me from behind or from a distance, why I smile a little vaguely because I have not been able to understand what they are saying. Honey comes to my rescue and, would you believe it, people sometimes talk to her and expect her to relay their words to me?"

A girl sitting in the third row said, "I have a good imagination, but I can't imagine what it would be like to be deaf."

A small voice near the rear said, "I can." She was wearing large dark glasses and her fingers were busy with a stylus making braille notes.

"What is it like?" someone asked.

"It is like living in a prison of silence and it can be very lonely," Willa replied. Her tone was gentle, her words matter of fact. "I was not always deaf and so when I see the branches of a tree moving, or stand by a lake where water laps the shore, I can remember what the sounds were like and they make a music in my mind."

"Do you watch TV?"

"Yes, when the words are printed with the picture or when someone off to one side is signing. That is how I learned about Hearing Ear Dogs. I saw them on a TV program."

The children were moved. Their questions went beyond curiosity into awareness of a whole other way of living, and from awareness into a desire to help.

A boy in the back row spoke up. "There are so many things

you can do for a blind person—read to them, offer help, guide them, cut up their food, what can we do for a deaf person?"

Willa's answer came slowly. "You can speak clearly, face the person directly, use your hands and facial expression to support your words—show them you care."

Rosey was bouncing up and down on her toes. She gave a signal and the class stood. Individually and together they all made the three signs Rosey had taught them, the signs that said "I love you."

The smile that had flickered occasionally on Willa's face became steady. In her voice that carried well she said, "That is the most important thing of all." She put her hand on Honey's head. "Honey shows what love is, what love can do."

An hour later, at home, Willa looked at Honey and laughed. "Do you know what we've just done? We've given a demonstration!"

The alarm was not set to go off on Sunday mornings, but often when Willa awoke she discovered Honey standing by her bed, tail gently waving, eyes looking at her; then joy when Willa finally hove herself out of the covers and her feet fumbled for her slippers. She closed the window, brushing away the slight accumulation of snow that had fallen during the night, then stood still watching the flakes as they drifted slowly down. No need to wonder if it was making any sound; she remembered from the time she was a little girl that snow was the quietest of nature's offerings, only a wind could make it swish, and there was no wind today.

"Honey, see what's waiting for you!" she exclaimed, going to the kitchen door and opening it.

For a moment Honey stood poised at the surprise, then she ran into the snow, pushed her nose along and through it, rolled and shook free, rolled again, then leaped and did one of her air somersaults. She was having such fun that she seemed to have forgotten the purpose of her being let out. Willa watched her, sharing the abandonment, remembering. When Willa finally called her in she came readily enough, eager for her breakfast. Willa rubbed her with a towel, then she dried one paw after another, reaching between the pads for snow. Honey relished the attention and lapped Willa's face.

Two letters were propped up on the kitchen table. They had come earlier in the week and Willa had saved them to answer on Sunday: one was from a service club, the other from a women's group in a neighboring town. Had they come a month ago, trepidation would have given her the only answer, "No, sorry." Since her afternoon at the school her only answer would be, "Yes, gladly." She looked down at Honey, "It will be your show."

Honey heard the knocking at the front door and went back and forth from it to Willa until she convinced Willa that it was not because she wanted to go out again in the snow but because someone wanted to come in. It was Denis, snow shovel in hand and behind him the front walk cleared and clean. Willa asked him to come in and Honey danced around him until he was sitting at the kitchen table drinking coffee and listening to Willa telling him about the two letters, asking him to read them. His response was what she had secretly hoped for, but it took her by surprise as it came so soon.

"I'll help, drive you there. Be handy for anything."

"Will you let me help you with the bundles of clothing tomorrow evening?"

"Indeed yes, Honey too."

He refused a second cup of coffee, with his eyes on the clock. "Service is at eleven. Coming with me? Honey may be the first dog ever inside St. Martin's, but if your work goes the way it's going she won't be the last."

Willa shook her head. "I haven't been in a church for years."

"Why?"

"Because—because . . ."

He intercepted her thought. "You don't go to church to hear or even to see, you go to be part of something—" he reached for the words that might be easy for her, "something beyond yourself that enfolds you."

When Honey saw her leash come down from its hook and felt Willa attaching it to her collar, she drew her tongue over Willa's hand in anticipation.

For a long time life had been like a straight road for Willa, one mile little different from another and no reason to think it would ever be different. She had learned to live within her restrictions, and if there was something called joy to find it in muted ways. Now life had become a road with views and vistas, turnings: no mile like the one already traversed.

That afternoon she replied to the two letters, agreeing to the arrangements already suggested and saying she would come with a friend who would help with some of the details. Daily practice with Honey, one trial run with Denis, and she felt ready for the first of the two successive Friday evenings. The meeting was in a hall large enough for chairs to be spaced comfortably with an open area at the front where Willa would work. Honey was taken off leash and began to wander at will among the audience. Willa nodded assent, knowing it was the only way Honey's responses could be natural and spontaneous.

The chairman made a brief introduction, then he spoke from notes Willa had given him about the program. "Miss Macy has requested that no matter how appealing Honey is, as she goes up to you one after another, that you do not give her any kind of tidbit. That can come later when we have refreshments. There are six basic sounds that every Hearing Ear Dog is trained to. Some people have special requirements; their dogs will be trained to them. How many sounds does Honey have now?"

Willa lifted six fingers. Honey was learning more but she did not want to put her through them tonight.

The chairman sat down and Willa went to the table where an alarm clock was clearly visible. She set it to go off in two minutes, then she stretched out on the couch that was near and closed her eyes as if in sleep. Honey was wandering around the room, greeting people with a lap of her tongue, a wag of her tail.

The alarm went off. She alerted, stood still for a moment, then raced past the people in the chairs, across the open space to stand beside the couch and push her nose against Willa's cheek. She nuzzled Willa until Willa got off the couch and embraced her. Everyone in the room heard her saying, "Good girl, such a good girl." On a nearby stand was a telephone. It began to ring loudly and persistently. Honey was not familiar with telephones, but she knew that any bell must be attended to, so she directed Willa to the phone.

There was a door at the far end of the hall and someone most certainly wanted to get in, as the knocking could be heard by everyone, especially Honey, who ran to the door then back to Willa. Together they went to the door. Willa opened it and Honey's ecstasy was unbounded when she saw who it was: Denis.

Then the smoke alarm screeched. It startled everyone and its insistency made some people nervous. Honey was the calmest in the room. She went to the sound, then to the nearest outside exit and there she waited. Willa realized what her moves meant and crossed the room to go to Honey. Putting her hand on the door she opened it and both went out. When the smoke alarm was silenced they returned to the room.

From the small kitchen where refreshments were being prepared a tea kettle started to whistle. Honey went to Willa who made no move, then she went to the kitchen and returned to Willa.

"She wants her to do something about it," a woman in the audience whispered loudly.

And Willa did. She followed Honey into the kitchen and turned the stove off.

"If there's nothing more, we will now adjourn for refreshments," the chairman said, then turned to thank Willa and commend Honey. But there was something more.

From a seat in the back row a baby started to cry. Honey, standing close beside Willa, looked up at her questioningly. Willa saw a young woman endeavoring to quiet her little one. She saw the small mouth opening widely, the tears sliding down the cheeks. Honey knew what to do, she ran to the sound then back to Willa. Her whole being, including the moving tail, was a question mark. Willa put her hand on the golden head, "Go," she said, shaping the word carefully, "do what you can."

And Honey did, returning to lap the baby's wet cheeks until a smile shone through the tears.

"She's never practiced that sound with me," Willa said to no one in particular.

And yet, perhaps she had.

A man in the front row stood up with an envelope in his hands. "We want to do something for the program. Would Honey help us here?"

Willa took Honey's head between her palms, then pointed to the man. Honey trotted over to him and took the envelope in her glove-soft lips. It was not even moist when she presented it to Willa. This was a first for Honey and she handled it with grace and dignity. Willa thought of the stories she had heard of how small Molly would race around a room and collect dollar bills, then race back to instructor or trainer.

The demonstration was over. Willa begged to be excused from the refreshments and Denis concurred, knowing that too much was asked of Willa to converse with people whose lips might be involved with eating. Honey was reluctant to leave, but a signal from Willa, a slight tug on the leash, and she submitted. She knew she had done what she was supposed to do. Words of admiration and hands reaching out to stroke her as she left the hall and went toward the car were her reward.

Denis drove up to a small restaurant that looked attractive as well as expensive, but for once, and on their first meal out, he would have gone to the Ritz had there been one. At the door they were met by a pleasant but firm host. "Sorry, but we do not allow dogs with our patrons. Please leave the animal in your car."

"This is a specially trained dog," Denis said.

Willa held out her ID with Honey's name and picture and the words of explanation that Hearing Ear Dogs must now be legally accepted in all public places. There was nothing for the host to do but admit them with a smile that was no smile. Honey kept close to Willa and tucked herself neatly under the table between two pairs of friendly legs.

"You're tired." It was not a question, it was a statement of fact.

Willa found it easy to reply. "Yes, always after I project my voice for any length of time, but I was proud of Honey. She really did it all."

"Not quite all, you touched them too, Willa."

"Talk to me, Denis. I'd always rather listen than talk."

"Even when listening demands concentration on your part?"

"Even then."

An hour later when they left, the host went to the door with them. "Your dog has behaved better than many of our patrons. Will you present this to her when you get home, with our compliments?"

In the bag handed her Willa felt the shape of a marrow bone.

HEARING EAR DOG PROGRAM

That was the heading on the letter Willa received early in the year, one that went out to all graduates.

Hi! Happy New Year to you from all of us at the program. Here is our annual survey which we use to follow up on your progress with your dog and to find out if there are any problems that we can help you solve. We would appreciate it if you could take time to answer the following questions. Your reply will help us evaluate our training program. Please complete and return the questionnaire by February 20. Thank you.

Pencil in hand, Willa took pleasure in answering the various questions, filling in first her name and then Honey's.

1. Is your dog responding to all the sounds that it was trained to do?
2. Have you taught your dog to respond to any new sounds?
3. Do you find that you have the time to practice every day? If not, how often do you practice?
4. How is your dog's basic obedience?
5. Do you take your dog to stores and restaurants?
6. Any other general comments?

Willa felt that one big affirmation answered all the questions. She was glad now that she had been asked to do the demonstrations, for they gave her examples in answer for the "general comments." What could she say except to describe how well Honey had done, almost too well, for she clearly liked to show off, and the attention she received was her delight. Willa could not resist a question of her own: What would happen to the world if we all acted out of love and were satisfied with love as our remuneration?

It was a letter that could be answered and returned long before the required date.

Four

It WAS A MILD EVENING, the first warm hint of spring was in the air, the windows were open and there was fragrance. Denis and Willa had been having supper together on Friday nights for several weeks, often at Willa's, occasionally going out to a restaurant. Their conversations filled blanks about each other's lives. Willa knew about Denis's parents, that they had died some time ago and that Mr. Locke had done much as a surrogate. Conscious of what Honey was doing for her, Willa longed to know what Pundit had done for Denis.

"Why Pundit?" she asked on that particular evening.

"He came with the name as a four-month-old pup, but he grew into it. He was a teacher by nature, perhaps all dogs are. We did everything together and he made himself as pleasing to my mother as to my father, so he was with me whatever my address. We were necessary to each other. I didn't matter much to my parents, except as a minor tax deduction. I did matter to Pundit. In my early teens our gang started doing some foolish things, not always bad but they could have had consequences. And did. There was one . . ." he turned away.

"Don't get off the track," Willa said, "keep on with the story."

Facing her again he smiled an apology and went on. "When I'd get home from one of our escapades Pundit would look at me with eyes that almost looked through me, so calm and wise, not exactly reproachful, but wondering. Why? He went to college with me, they let me keep him in the dorm. By the time I graduated he was beginning to show his years. I resented that, because the years at college were fitting me for living. That was when I began to let him teach me, since I saw through him what time did to life.

"I resisted, he accepted. Tranquillity for Pundit was a warm place in the sun or a cool place in the shade. He kept his head up and his gaze was always forward, as if he saw things that I couldn't see. Then, one day last summer . . ." Denis turned away but continued talking.

Willa leaned toward him and put her hands gently on his cheeks, turning his face back to her. "I want to have it all. We've shared the richness, now we must the share the other. It will be so for me someday, and Honey."

With words coming inevitably like sands through an hour glass, he told her of the day that he knew had to be his last with Pundit. "He was a great age by then, sixteen. Sight had dimmed, and hearing. In rain or snow he easily became disoriented, and he did not move with freedom. He had given me a reason to live and I, because it was the one last gift I had for him, gave him the means to die. The vet told me what to do. My heart was aching, but something in me was soaring—a life lived nobly could die nobly, and by the hand of the one who had been loved and served."

Denis came to the end of his story, realizing that Willa's eyes had not left his face. "I've never said this before. No one has ever listened to me the way you do."

"It's what I can do."

"I've needed someone to listen to me."

"I've needed someone to talk to me."

Denis put his head in his hands. Willa sat back in her chair, aware of something so blessed that there were no words for it. They had shared much during the past months, as they grew to know each other; now they were sharing sorrow. She did not want to reach out and touch his hands, or do what she had not yet done, embrace him. It would look as if she was offering comfort or pity, and those he did not need.

Honey had been near the window of the house where the scents and sounds of the warm evening were. There had been no reason for her to be alert, but she had not been asleep. Scarcely making a sound, she crossed the room to stand beside Denis's chair, then with sure motions she lapped his face, slowly, softly, giving her love in the way she had to give it and asking nothing in return.

Some time later when Denis said good-bye standing in the doorway, his arms went around Willa. Her arms found their way. Their lips met. He could not speak; she would not have heard.

The first Monday evening of the month had become part of the pattern of living. Willa and Honey, returning from work, had a brief play time in the backyard and an early supper, then Willa changed into jeans and shirt and with Honey met Denis on the porch at St. Martin's at seven o'clock. The days were longer now and their work could be done in daylight; the piles were getting bigger, as if people were cleaning out their too-used clothes or not-enough-used winter clothes to get ready for another season.

"The usual," Denis commented as he gestured to the accumulation: some bundles of neatly folded clean clothes, others scarcely worth looking at.

Invariably Denis found something for Honey, and this time he held up a pair of cut-down shorts, paint stained and torn, but with a splendid zipper. He tossed it to Honey who raced off with it to work on. She soon left the shorts and went to a pile of rejects left in a corner and began rooting around in it.

She stood still for a moment, cocked her head, then went to Willa and nudged her. Willa gave her a pat, used to Honey's moments when all she seemed to want was recognition, but this was different. Honey went back to the pile, nosed it, then returned to Willa.

Denis said, "Why is she barking?"

"I can see she is, that means attention."

Denis looked at the pile. "Sounds as if a cricket was down in there. We'll get to it in a few minutes."

"Is May the month for crickets?" Willa asked. "Honey is telling me something. I can't put her off any longer." Willa left the sorting she was doing and went to the pile of miscellaneous oddments. Honey watched her, wagging her tail, pleased as she always was when she got her message through.

Willa's hands fumbled in the pile. "Why, it's an alarm clock, with a knobby sock attached to it, and it's still ticking! Good girl."

Suddenly Denis was by her side. Seizing the clock and the sock that looked as if it had been stuffed with an assortment of oddly shaped balls, he threw it as far as he could across the lawn, laying a restraining hand on Honey so she wouldn't chase it. "It's not a clock, it's a little bomb." He turned to face Willa and repeated his words. "It didn't get in with the clothes, it was put in. Did you see what time the alarm was set for?"

Willa had. "Eight-thirty."

The church clock above them had only recently struck eight. "We've time to put it out of commission. Keep Honey while I get some water to dowse it with, then I'll bury it."

Willa sat down on the porch steps and held Honey close to her as she watched Denis approach the innocent looking clock with its stuffed sock tail. He poured two pails of water on it, used his knife to detach the clock, then dug a hole for the rest and stamped the earth down over it. When he came back he sat beside Willa and gave Honey the praise she fed on.

"You just thought it was a new kind of Frisbee, good girl." He turned full-face to Willa. "It was a very little bomb, it could not have done much harm, perhaps started a small fire just after we had left—if it hadn't been discovered."

"But why? But who?"

Denis held out his hands, palms up, a gesture well known between them that took the place of words. "A prank, but sometimes a prank can have consequences." He rolled the clock over and studied it. "I think I know who did this. I'll try to have a talk with him."

"But why, something against the church?"

"Not the church—life, the world, and he thinks he can make a protest this way. I could have done something like this once."

"And that's why you want to work to keep youngsters from doing things like this?"

"Much more. Divert their energies into constructive channels. What seems a prank, and that's all this alarm clock is, could have serious consequences."

"Consequences." Willa repeated the last word. "Like what?"

Denis was silent, moving his head slowly.

"Like what?" she reminded him of her question.

He faced her at the beginning as he told her of some of the escapades he and his gang had engaged in, but more often he looked ahead of him and Willa missed his words. She did not care. Once she laid her hand on his knee and said, "It's you now, Denis, that I know. I don't need to be told about the things you did and that are far behind you."

He shook his head. "I want you to know." His lips, usually so mobile, were tightly set and even when he faced her she did not get his words clearly, but it seemed to be something he needed to say and the word "consequences" kept coming through to her.

In the silences between them and in her loss of some of his words, Willa went back to something she had put out of her mind but could never forget—the time when a firecracker had been tied to her pigtail. Consequences. It was never known who did it, but had she wanted to she could have told Denis that she knew something about consequences. The person who did it most likely did not know her, had nothing against her; it was a prank, it would make a big noise. Those who had been near reported that a group of hoodlums had run off laughing, disappearing into the crowd gathered for a Fourth of July celebration.

In a gesture that she had not used for years, Willa put her hand up to the back of her head the way she used to when she wore a pigtail.

Denis did not see her; his head was in his hands and the last word she was aware of his saying was "regret."

"But it's regret that has made you want to do something with your life," she said softly.

He nodded.

"Then perhaps it was worth it."

Willa stared ahead of her, lost in her own remembering. She did not see the tears that were travelling slowly down Denis's cheeks, nor the sobs that shook him, revealing what a torturous journey back into the past of his misdeeds he had had to make. There was nothing Willa could do, but Honey knew what was needed. She licked Denis's face and made whimpering sounds. He put his arm around her and drew her to him. Willa's arm had been circling Honey, and their hands met, then their eyes.

"I've been trying to tell you these things about me for a long time."

"And I wouldn't listen. It doesn't matter, Denis, it's what you are now, what you have ahead of you to do."

"With your help."

The clock in the tower above them struck the half hour, the hands of the alarm clock were in agreement, but neither sound nor movement came from the small harmless mound where the earth looked fresh. Darkness was coming down. Denis put the pails and shovel away. Willa straightened the tumbled pile that had held the clock. Honey waited patiently. It was one of the times when she was not needed, so she sat still, ready for the signal to move whenever it should come.

There was something inevitable about their relationship. It had existed from the day when Honey's brief excursion into the big world had terminated in her returning with, or being returned by, Denis; it was never quite clear which way it was. After their first hesitancy, Willa and Denis had begun to enjoy discovering each other. They had helped each other. They had shared deep thoughts. Willa could agree with Mr. Locke that Denis was indeed "a nice young fellow," but he was becoming so much more.

As the weeks and months went on and winter had yielded to spring and spring to the future, part of the inevitability was that they should make plans.

"I will have the degree I'm working for in June."

"And then?"

"Then I want to have an office of my own and be available to young people who need to talk, who need someone to listen."

"How will you find them?"

"I'll go to schools and visit with teachers. There are many young people to whom I'll make the approach myself."

Willa thought back to her own troubled teens, wondering what it would have meant if there had been someone with whom she could talk. She knew she might not have been able to listen well then, but it was not that so much as being able to talk.

There were often long silences between Willa and Denis that nurtured conversation. It gave time to think between ideas, to see what happened as they lay in the mind, to bring forth a well-burnished response, and then go on.

"June," Willa repeated the word, saying it slowly. The thought brought forth the feeling of warm days, the sight of flowers and their growing, the smell of mown grass. There would be birds, and she could hear their songs inwardly when she watched the vibrations of their throats.

Again there was a silence.

"I've asked for my two weeks vacation the last part of June. That's when the Dog Show is being held. It will be a reunion for Honey's class. There will be other dogs from other classes."

"I'd like to drive you and Honey there."

Thinking of June and all that it meant for each of them, they went a step further into all that it might mean for them both. Willa was still hesitant of anything that brought her too much before people.

"Not a big church," she said, so softly that Denis just caught the words.

"The town clerk has more than dog licenses."

Willa smiled with relief, then she beamed, "Something quiet and plain." She slipped her hand into Denis's.

"But no less real and binding."

"Shall we say bonding? I've learned to love that word."

Willa had the better part of a week to think of what was impending in her life, for Denis would be away until Saturday. With only Honey to confide in, she began to have misgivings. Was it being fair, she asked herself, to burden Denis with her problem, to impose her deafness on so young a man whose life was before him, whose career was in his hands? He wanted to learn to sign and she would teach him, but it was difficult and a long time before one became adept. She compelled herself to think of all they could not share—listening to music, watching a play unless it was miming. And her own voice, which she did not hear herself, modulated by the implant she wore in one ear—wouldn't he grow tired in time of that one tone? It devastated her to think of these things, but she felt she must face them and find her own answers.

"Honey, Honey, what should I do?"

She could withdraw, see him once more and then never

again; he would disagree, but in the end it might be better to hurt him now than have a hurt go through his whole life.

Honey often sensed when Willa was deep in troubling thoughts. Now, as she had done before, she placed herself in front of Willa and their eyes held each other. Willa talked on in a murmuring way. Honey listened and eventually drew her tongue across the back of Willa's hand.

"You're right, Honey, we've gone far enough and I'm getting nowhere; let's go for a walk in the park."

Willa hoped to see Rosey and she did, but it was a different Rosey who came running across the grass with no eyes for anyone but Honey.

"I need you Honey," she said as she dropped down beside Honey and wrapped her arms about her.

Willa did not hear the words, but the attitude told her enough. She went to the bench where they had so often sat to talk and read and sign together, knowing that when Rosey had shared her secret or sorrow or shame or whatever it was with Honey, she would join her.

And she did.

"I needed to talk to someone who wouldn't talk back to me," Rosey announced as she sat down beside Willa and pushed her hair back from her face.

The story came out in breathless haste, and though Willa did not get it all, as Rosey often forgot to look at her but addressed herself to Honey or to the wide open air, Willa got enough to know that it was a minor tragedy. Rosey had broken a china horse belonging to her best friend.

"And she thought I did it on purpose—" and then a gasp as Rosey tried to say how it happened. "And she kept talking back so fast that I couldn't explain—" then a struggle with a sob, "And I needed someone who wouldn't talk back and there was Honey." She threw her arms around Willa, "You'll listen, won't you, and let me tell how it happened?"

"I'll listen," Willa said, and in a flash of time the scene

changed and she saw herself saying those very words to Denis when he came home of an evening needing to have someone listen to him, someone with whom his words would be safe and sacrosanct. She returned Rosey's embrace. "We all need each other, Rosey, and perhaps we should be able to say that more often than we do."

They talked about other things, they did some signing, and for lack of a Frisbee Rosey threw sticks for Honey, who raced gleefully in pursuit and retrieval. When it was time to go their separate ways, Willa took Rosey's hands in hers and looked at her as she looked at Honey, eyes searching eyes. "Just say two very simple words when you see your friend Patsy again, 'I'm sorry.' She'll listen."

"Do you really think so?"

"I really do."

Willa had Saturday chores to do, but the one that lightened the day was preparing supper. Denis would be back in town by six o'clock with news of his finals and more plans for the future. He would look at her in a way that said as clearly as any words "All is well, isn't it?" And she would reply, "All is well." She could not account to herself how it was that her misgivings had vanished. All she knew was that a simple equation had been worked out: she needed him and he needed her. In admitting something that had grown between them almost without their knowing it, they would acknowledge a debt each owed the other.

A few weeks later in the town clerk's office, with Honey beside them, they raised their right hands and made their promises. As with so much that had happened during the past months, it was as simple as that.

Once home, Willa was eager to have Denis see the new word she had been teaching Honey.

"I'm going to our room and shall close the door, or almost close it. It's an arrangement Honey and I have had for a long time. She knows I do not need her for awhile and amuses herself. After a few minutes, call her to you, take her head in your hands, look at her earnestly, and ask her to find Mrs. Talcot."

Willa left and went to the other room, partly closing the door. Denis let several minutes go by then he called Honey, looked into her eyes and said, "Go, find Mrs. Talcot."

Honey seemed uncertain. She turned her head one way then another only to see that there was no familiar person in the room with them. She looked back at Denis, searching his face. He repeated the words.

Suddenly, with a flash of movement and a tail wagging enough to propel her body, she swung around and ran to the half-open door. She pushed it with her nose, saw Willa, and hurled herself against her.

"Thank you, Honey, that's a good girl." Willa's praise was lavish. "Now, go back to Denis."

Honey whirled around and ran to throw herself against him.

Denis did not need Willa's careful directions about the various turns in the road as they approached the place where the Dog Show was being held. The dogs already there were making their presences heard, and a medley of barks filled the air. Rounding the last turn, they drove into the parking space. Willa attached the leash to Honey's collar, and Honey had all the indication she needed that from this moment on she would be working. Denis saw the chairs on the lawn where onlookers were gathering and found a place among them, while Willa and Honey went off to join the score or more of dogs all bonded to their owners, all proclaiming what they were by their yellow harnesses and leashes.

People were talking together, renewing friendships: those who were speech readers silently, those who were signers gesticulating, those who could benefit by hearing aids audibly. Instructors and trainers moved among them all, talking and signing. Willa had caught the instructor's eye as she and Denis had come across the lawn, and the warmth of the smile that embraced them gave her an assurance that went beyond words. There was no time for talk, though there would be later. This was the time when attention was on the dogs.

"How's Emily?"

"Fantastic! I fractured my leg last fall and had it in a cast, but she adjusted her pace to mine. Once I tripped and lost my cane, but Emily picked it up and gave it to me. At night she carries my flashlight."

"And Cookie?"

"There never was such a dog! She even heard a mouse nibbling in the cupboard and told me to do something about it."

"Laddie?"

"Not always good on the alarm clock, because he knows once he wakes me I'll soon be leaving him. He still has a lot to learn about names as he confuses Debbie with Daddy."

"Jack?"

"He's a miracle dog, does everything and much more, but he does oversleep once or twice a week."

"And Ebony?"

"She took second in an Obedience Class and is on her way with points toward a C.D.—Companion Dog."

"And Honey?"

"She saved my life from loneliness." There was so much more for Willa to say, but it was time to move on to the events.

"We told you it was a working partnership and a growing process. I'm proud of you all," the instructor said. "Now, into the ring and line up with dogs from some of the other classes. There are prizes for all the firsts."

Denis, sitting on the lawn that sloped down to the ring, was in the midst of similar approbation as friends and families talked about what the dogs had done in their homes.

"Nugget gave Joan back her life with her unselfish love."

"Our boy couldn't seem to make friends in school, but Captain made them for him, and now he's tops in everything."

"Our house would have burned down if Kelpie hadn't discovered the stove was on and woke my wife. Neighbors heard the barking, but it took more than barking, and Kelpie knew it."

"It's love in action, that's all you can say about these dogs."

In the ring the parade formed. Dogs and their owners walked slowly around so the audience could see the participants and the judges could begin their determinations. Denis, reading the program, felt sure that Honey would win every class.

Best Groomed came first and, though Honey's coat shone and her feathers had been neatly trimmed, the prize went to another dog. Then came Basic Obedience. Honey did all she was asked to do but she was slow on the "down" command because she was too interested in all that was going on around her. She did not even place for a first in Special Tricks as Jack outran, outleaped, and outsomersaulted her in Frisbee catching. She did not shine as Superdog. This was a test to demonstrate steadiness and control in different situations. She had held back at one of the obstacles and stood in front of Willa, blocking her way; not sure herself, she would not impose an unknown on her owner.

The last class was for Best Tail Wag and the program indicated that dogs would be judged on technique, rhythm, and style. Honey's tail never stopped wagging, it went up and down, crosswise and even turned like a clock hand. The award went to a small dog whose tail never lost momentum but was always in perfect rhythm.

There was one class left. It was the sum of all the classes and had been viewed throughout the competition by judges and trainers as they determined what dog had improved most during the year since training. Again the participants lined up, dogs at heel, handlers standing quietly, reaching down to stroke a head or murmur a proud word or a comforting word.

The instructor stepped forward to make the announcements, signing and speaking. "This is, perhaps, the most important of the awards as it shows what has been happening between one person and one dog during the past year. There is no question in the minds of judges and trainers but that the one showing the most improvement is Honey."

Honey heard her name before Willa caught the significance and stepped forward, drawing Willa with her.

"And Willa, of course," the instructor said as she presented the trophy to the surprised and delighted Willa. Speaking to everyone present, as well as to Willa, the instructor continued, "We were not entirely sure when we matched you two last summer, because Honey needed someone to whom she could be all and everything, and that is not always possible in every household. Only by being totally responsible would Honey be able to show the confidence so needed in a Hearing Ear Dog."

Willa's smile, often so fleeting, did not fade. "But it's Honey who has given *me* confidence."

"Then you both deserve the award, and it proves that our decision was right."

The participants clapped, the onlookers clapped, the dogs barked. Willa and Honey, now free and proud of their trophy, went to join Denis.

They watched as recognition was given to many different people and various organizations who were making the program possible by their sponsorship. Then there was a picnic with the kind of food that owners could share with their dogs. There was much talk and laughter, with assurances made to each other that they would meet again at the next Dog Show, and then it was time for good-byes.

When, at last, Willa and Denis went to the car, Honey crawled in and flattened out on the back seat. She was tired and she didn't care who knew it. It had been a big day for her, and there was no longer any need to be on duty. She opened one eye, saw that Denis was in the driver's seat, and closed it again. She did not have to help him drive.

The instructor, watching them drive off, turned to the two trainers standing beside her and smiled.

One of the trainers said, "That was a good match."

The other said, "That *is* a good match."